*New Jersey and
the Revolutionary War*

The Battle of Princeton

Washington's arrival turns the tide on January 3, 1777. From a painting by James Peale.
Courtesy of Princeton University Library

New Jersey and
the Revolutionary War

ALFRED HOYT BILL

RUTGERS UNIVERSITY PRESS
New Brunswick, New Jersey

COPYRIGHT © 1964, BY
THE NEW JERSEY TERCENTENARY COMMISSION

Library of Congress Cataloging in Publication Data

Bill, Alfred Hoyt, 1879–
  New Jersey and the Revolutionary War.

  Original ed. issued as v. 11 of The New Jersey historical
series.
  Includes bibliographical references.
  1. New Jersey—History—Revolution. I. Title.
II. Series: The New Jersey historical series, v. 11.
E263.N5B5   1971   974.9′03   72–8066

ISBN 0–8135–0642–5

PRINTED IN THE UNITED STATES OF AMERICA

PREFACE

Two features of the story of New Jersey and the Revolutionary War have been hitherto less emphasized than they should be. One is the fact that, although New Jersey has been well called the Cockpit of the Revolution, it was far more than merely the theater of operations that proved to be decisive. The other is that although the war had something of the character of a civil war in all the rebellious colonies outside of New England, this was conspicuously so in New Jersey.

In several districts the Loyalists were in the majority. The presence of the British army at New York and on Staten Island and the British warships in the Hudson, for seven of the eight years of the war, made loyalty to the Crown as popular as it was safe in neighboring Bergen and Essex counties. Opportunities for trading with the enemy stimulated the activities of the "Pine Robbers" in Monmouth County. The remoteness of much of the West Jersey country, and the numerous Quakers among the inhabitants, limited that district's inclination toward revolution.

Elsewhere in the State, however, Patriot feeling predominated; and one reads of no place where the arrival of British forces was hailed as a deliverance. It has been stated that there were as many battalions of Jerseymen in the service of the British Crown as in the Continental

Army, but those battalions had to be formed in New York of Loyalists who had made their devious ways through the lines to join them.

It was the support of the civilian population, tardy though it was, that made the terrible winter at Morristown endurable for General Washington's army. New Jersey militia kept Sir William Howe's army cooped up at New Brunswick and Amboy, dependent on river-borne supplies from New York in the winter after the Trenton-Princeton campaign. They had a great part in stopping Howe's advance on Philadelphia the following summer. By their labor they contributed greatly to the defense of the forts on the Delaware. The crying needs of Washington's army at Valley Forge so drained New Jersey's resources that Governor William Livingston was moved to protest to Washington against further calls upon the State. When Sir Henry Clinton's army retired across the State from Philadelphia to New York the following summer, the populace fled before it, taking with them their cattle and possessions, down to the ropes and buckets from their wells. Farmers and militia joined the Continentals at the battle of Springfield in defeating the last serious military operation by the British in New Jersey.

But the principal campaigns of which the State was the theater tend to monopolize the student's attention, and deserve to do so, for they were a brilliant and dramatic as their results were decisive. Without Washington's recovery of the initiative in the Trenton-Princeton campaign it seems the war must have been forever lost. His patient maneuvering throughout the following summer made possible General Horatio Gates' victory at Saratoga. The desperate tenacity with which he maintained his position at Valley Forge made the possession of Philadelphia valueless to the enemy. The battle at Monmouth Court House proved that, at long last, American troops could outfight the British in open field.

Three years later, at the dinner that Washington gave

for the captured British officers after the surrender at Yorktown, Lord Cornwallis, in a speech of chivalrous generosity, made quite clear his understanding of New Jersey's importance in the war:

> When the illustrious part that your Excellency has borne in the long and arduous contest becomes a matter of history, fame will gather your brightest laurels rather from the banks of the Delaware than from those of the Chesapeake.

For their careful reading of my manuscript and their many valuable suggestions regarding it, my hearty thanks go to Messrs. John T. Cunningham, Richard P. McCormick, Gordon B. Turner, Richard M. Huber, Wheaton J. Lane, and to the staff members of the Tercentenary Commission.

ALFRED HOYT BILL

Princeton, New Jersey
June, 1964

vii

CONTENTS

LIST OF ILLUSTRATIONS

I

A TIME THAT TRIED MEN'S SOULS

"T HE CONDUCT OF THE JERSEYS has been most infamous." So, on December 18, 1776, wrote General George Washington to his brother John Augustine. He wrote very much in the mood of the Psalmist who said in his haste, "all men are liars"; and with his unfailing sense of justice Washington wrote in another letter that same day, "The defection of the people in the lower part of Jersey has been mostly due to the want of an army to look the enemy in the face." For, actually, the Jerseys had done their full part for the Patriot cause from the meeting of their Provincial Congress in the summer of 1775 until the landing of a British army on their soil eighteen months later. But in the behavior of their people in the previous four weeks and in the situation to which that behavior had reduced the Commander in Chief of the Continental Armies there was some justification for his outburst against them.

He wrote from the Pennsylvania side of the Delaware River, to which he and the remnants of his army had escaped only by the grace of General William Howe's leisurely pursuit of them. The four-month campaign that had begun in August had been little better than a series of defeats, retreats, and disasters. The battle of Long Island had been lost, New York abandoned, Fort Washington taken by assault, and Fort Lee, with its artillery and great store of supplies, evacuated only just in time to save its garrison from capture. In the retreat across New Jersey that followed, New Jersey regiments, their enlistments expired, marched home, though not one regiment of New Jersey militia responded to the call to defend their home-country. Since then, with British and Hessian garrisons dominating the country from Perth Amboy through New Brunswick and Princeton to the Delaware, Jersey citizens had been flocking to British posts to receive pardon for their rebellion and renew their allegiance to King George III.

The Jerseys had not been like that when Washington had ridden across them a year and a half before to take command of the troops besieging General Howe's army in Boston. That summer the Provincial Congress, with its Committees of Safety and Observation, had supplanted the royal government and was holding the colony sternly to the Continental cause. By the following summer (1776) revolutionary sentiment had become dominant. But the Jerseys lacked the political consciousness and the solidarity of opposition to the Crown that years of wrangling with tyrannical royal governors had forged in New England. Nor had the Jerseys New England's homogeneity of population, of education, and of religion; and they had no such united leadership as New England had.

At Perth Amboy, the actual capital, although Burlington enjoyed the same titular rank, officers of the Crown and merchants who had grown rich in trade with the other North American colonies and the West Indies lived elegantly in fine houses staffed by numerous Negro slaves, and attended services of the Church of England. Thrifty Dutch farmers, with snug, one-story dwellings and great stone barns, cultivated much of the north of Bergen and Essex counties and clung to the Dutch Reformed Church of their forefathers. Congregationalist New Englanders had settled New Ark and Elizabeth Town and become Presbyterians. For, although there were many Quaker settlements scattered throughout the Colony, and a number of Anglican parishes, the people were mostly followers of John Knox and John Calvin.

Within the northern and western boundaries, where the widely scattered settlers led a frontier life, the hill country of Morris, Bergen, and Sussex counties was the domain of the opulent iron masters, whose miners and furnace and forge workmen lived close to poverty. At the other end of the Colony, where the Great Cedar Swamp cut the Cape May country off from the rest of the province, an enterprising population prospered at shipbuilding, whaling, cattle raising, and, not least, smuggling, for which a center was maintained by a group of Philadelphia merchants.

Farther up the Delaware, in the most thickly settled part of the Colony, numerous Swedish farmers, descendants of the settlers of New Sweden, tilled the soil with their own hands in spite of their accumulated wealth. Market boats carried on a brisk trade with Philadelphia, and Greenwich and Salem were ports of local importance. Between Trenton and Princeton and along the upper Raritan most of the rich agricultural country was divided into large farms that were worked by Negro slaves and owned by men of English descent whom an English traveler described as "literally gentlemen farmers." At least one such farmer kept a pack of fox hounds and hunted the fox as the planters did in Virginia.

But although they differed much in origin, wealth, and religion, foreign travelers found the Jersey people generally admirable for what they described as "the modest pride of the independant man who sees nothing above him but the laws and who knows neither the vanity, nor the prejudices, nor the servility of our European societies." And Jonathan Belcher, who became a Royal governor after having lived some sixty years in New England, thought it "the best country I have seen for men of middling fortunes and people who have to live by the sweat of their brows."

The Colony had been fortunate in its most recent governors. Belcher, who was governor from 1747 to 1757, had the colonial point of view and was altogether given to good works. Francis Bernard, who succeeded him, took pride in the harmony he managed to maintain between the Assembly and the other branches of the government during his two years in office. Governor William Franklin, son of Benjamin Franklin, whose term of office began in 1762, acted with great tact and discretion where conflict between the Royal authority and local interests threatened: the Cape May smugglers, for instance, even when apprehended, generally went unpunished. But he had fallen heir to discontents which it was beyond his power to assuage.

With the end of the French and Indian War and the removal of British troops from the Colony there had come a deep economic depression. The elaboration of the British mercantile system, with its restriction of the grain trade and other commerce with the West Indies, had brought distress to the farmers and a desperate shortage of currency for ordinary business transactions: in vain did Benjamin Franklin, the Colonies' agent in London, urge the home government to permit them to issue a currency of their own.

The Jerseys became a creditors' world in which debtors worth a thousand pounds could lose their farms for want of the cash to pay a debt of a hundred. The resulting litigation, moreover, revealed confusion in land titles that were often already complicated by grants of the old Dutch government or by purchases from the Indians, and it made a perfect field for speculation.

Popular indignation against these abuses had broken out in mob violence. There were barn burnings by "Liberty Boys" in several localities in 1769 and 1770. Also in 1770 the Assembly's plan for an issue of Colonial currency was rejected by the home government, and "Liberty and Property" became the watchword. The Stamp Act and the Mutiny Act created a general resentment by raising the issue of taxation without representation and thereby prevented the conflict between debtors and creditors from degenerating into a class war. Early in 1774 the students at Princeton burned their college's supply of tea, and that November a "Tea Party" down at Greenwich reflected the violence and lawlessness of the famous one at Boston.

Naturally most of the wealthy men of the Colony sided with the established order. They feared greatly for their holdings as talk of independence and a republic became more and more general. The more timid of them left the Colony during 1775, and most of those who stayed refrained from all open political action. There were, however, notable exceptions among the privileged.

Richard Stockton, of Princeton, one of the wealthiest men in New Jersey, expressed the opinion that Parliament had no legal authority over the Colonies so long as they were not represented in it, and proposed that they be represented in it by men of their own choosing. Like other young lawyers of his day, he had grown up under the influence of the liberal political thought of the eighteenth century. He strongly urged the Colony's sending representatives to the Stamp Act Congress; and although he was a member of the Governor's Council and had lately been made a judge of the provincial supreme court, he joined Elias Boudinot and William Alexander—generally known and remembered as Lord Stirling because of his claim to a lapsed Scottish earldom—in the movement to send delegates to the Second Continental Congress.

Among other men of wealth who shared his views

were John Stevens, Francis Hopkinson, and William Livingston, though Stevens and Hopkinson, like Stockton, were members of the Governor's Council. Their abilities, backed by their wealth and position, made them natural leaders, and many members of the Assembly, sheriffs, county judges, and justices of the peace followed where they led. By midsummer, 1775, they and their associates had organized a Provincial Congress, which took over control of the militia and, gradually, through local committees, the other functions of government.

With the news from Concord and Lexington, the Colony had gone military. Students at Princeton formed a military company to train them for commissions in the regiments the Provincial Congress was raising for the continental service. The Colony became gay with uniforms and the music of fifes and drums. By fall the First New Jersey Continental Regiment was guarding the shore opposite Staten Island, with headquarters at Elizabeth Town. The following spring three such battalions— poorly officered and disciplined, to be sure, and sadly lacking in clothes and even shoes—were helping General Philip Schuyler guard the invasion route from Canada by way of Lake Champlain; and a large part of the militia had been sent to defend New York, when it became clear that control of the Hudson would be the next objective of General Howe's army, which had passed the winter at Halifax after its evacuation of Boston.

Privateering had begun as early as the fall of 1775 and, by the following spring, had become a major Patriot activity along the Jersey coast, with headquarters at Little Egg Harbor. That January a British army supply ship had been captured off Sandy Hook and its cargo sold publicly at Elizabeth Town. At Greenwich in May a British warship's attempt to raid the coast for cattle was easily repulsed. Most successful of all was the episode of the brig *Nancy* down at Cape May in June.

Laden with arms and powder that the Continental Congress had purchased at St. Croix and St. Thomas and hotly pursued by six British men-of-war, her master ran her ashore in a fog, managed to land most of her cargo in friendly hands, and abandoned her before the fog lifted. He left a mine in her cabin, with a slow match burning, and no sooner had she been captured by boats from the pursuing ships than she blew up, hurling the boarding party "forty or fifty yards into the air," to the great satisfaction of Patriot observers. It was June 29, the day that the transports of General Howe's army, with their attendant warships, dropped anchor off Sandy Hook.

The last of the old New Jersey colonial assemblies had met in November, 1775. Since then, without a single warship or one soldier to support his authority, Governor Franklin had been able to do no more than live on in his official residence at Perth Amboy and strive to keep up some semblance of royal government. The preceding May he had written to his superiors in London that the Colonies would never submit to taxation except by their own chosen representatives and he had urged the calling of a congress at which they could discuss their grievances with commissioners appointed by the Crown. But the English government had persisted in its policy of coercion.

In January, 1776, he had suspended Lord Stirling from the Council for helping the Provincial Congress organize its troops. Stirling had retaliated by placing the Governor under arrest, with sentinels from those same troops at his door. Franklin was promptly released on the intercession of the chief justice; but when, in May, he issued a proclamation convoking the Assembly for a June session, the Provincial Congress voted him "an enemy of the liberties of his country" and had him brought before them at Burlington for examination. There, when he refused to answer their questions, he was subjected—representative though he was of the King to whom they still professed allegiance—to a bitter denunciation by the Reverend Doctor John Witherspoon, who was not above taunting him with his illegitimate birth. He was then sent as a prisoner to Connecticut, where he remained until he was exchanged two years later.

Doctor Witherspoon, President of the College of New Jersey, had long been strong for American Independence. That spring he had spoken ardently for it at a meeting in New Brunswick. Only four of the 36 men present had supported him in the vote that had followed his speech. But the feeling in the Colony had changed greatly within these few months, and that of the Provincial Congress had changed with it. Separation from the mother country was still regarded as a last resort, but by the end of June, with Howe's army about to land on Staten Island and large numbers of reinforcements known to be en route from England, no other course seemed open—short of abject submission.

The Provincial Congress sent Abraham Clark, John Hart, Francis Hopkinson, Richard Stockton, and John Witherspoon to represent the Colony at the Continental Congress in Philadelphia, and on July 4 the vote of New Jersey was cast for Independence. Two days before that, moreover, Jersey men had taken the decisive step for themselves: they had adopted a new constitution that declared an end to all civil authority under the Crown and called for the election of a new assembly and legislative council to meet the following month. On July 18 the Provincial Congress changed its name to the Convention of the State of New Jersey and made an oath, abjuring allegiance to King George III and pledging loyalty to the new government, a qualification for serving in the Assembly or Council.

This action was supported by the people generally.

But meanwhile the Tories—the Loyalists, as they were proud to call themselves—had become increasingly active. In some parts of the Colony they were both numerous and bold. In June militia had to be sent to suppress open violence in Hunterdon County. At Shrewsbury Tories had refused to form a Committee of Inspection, as directed by the Provincial Congress, until they were forced to do so by their neighbors at Freehold and elsewhere: and then they gave only lip service.

By July Monmouth County teemed with plots to assist the British invaders. Armed parties of "Pine Robbers," as the Patriots called them, lurked among the pines and dunes along the coast, keeping in touch with landing parties from the British ships, supplying them with information about Patriot numbers and movements, helping their foraging parties, and making life dangerous for the Patriot detachments that were assigned to guard the coast and drive the cattle inland out of the reach of foragers.

Working secretly for the same cause and cooperating with them indirectly were a few wealthy Loyalists who had not left the Colony. Among them they managed to raise six battalions that served with the British army throughout the war; their recruits in groups of thirty or forty from time to time broke across the lines for enlistment and organization under the British flag.

Helping in this endeavor and other Loyalist schemes was Courtland Skinner, attorney general under the Crown and a man of great wealth. One of Governor Franklin's last official acts was making Skinner a major general of New Jersey's Loyalist troops. When his machinations were finally discovered through the capture of one of his letters to British headquarters, he managed to make his escape to a British warship. Other prominent Tories were arrested and deported or restricted to their homes; and steps were taken for the sequestration

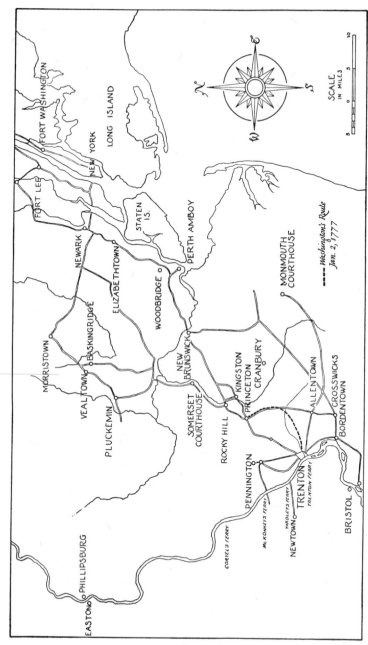

The Theater of Operations in New Jersey

From the author's *The Campaign of Prin...*

of the property of those who fled to the British. Tory-hunting became a popular pastime in some sections. There was tar-and-feathers for some conspicuous champions of the old order; and here and there, undoubtedly, an old grudge was settled under what passed for Patriot zeal.

With the arrival of the British in the Lower Bay fear of invasion had spread through the State. Most of the militia were in New York, under Washington's command, and there was little ammunition for the rest. The tents of Howe's troops on Staten Island were clearly visible across the water from Perth Amboy, and that town was bombarded when Patriot troops fired on some small boats loaded with British soldiers. Howe's purpose was clear: the capture of New York and control of the Hudson River in order to cut off the less unanimously revolutionary colonies from New England, the hotbed of rebellion. With that accomplished, his road would run straight across New Jersey to Philadelphia, the rebel capital.

Washington had had Manhattan and the opposite shores heavily fortified, since the island would become a trap for its defenders if the surrounding waterways were not closed to enemy warships. Redoubts and batteries guarded the water front; and these were supported by an entrenched camp on the Brooklyn shore and a battery garrisoned by New Jersey troops at Paulus Hook on the Jersey side. Upstream, a little below the entrance to the Harlem River, a heavy obstruction barred the Hudson's channel between Fort Washington and Fort Lee, whose heavy guns were fondly expected to close the river above them to the passage of enemy ships.

To protect his sources of supply in New Jersey and secure the road by which reinforcements could reach him from the south, Washington established what he called a "Flying Camp," under the command of General Hugh Mercer, with headquarters near Perth Amboy. As many as 10,000 militia from Pennsylvania, Maryland, and Delaware were gathered there by the middle of July. The Jersey militia who had been on duty in New York were held there for a time before being allowed to go home. Continental regiments from the southern colonies rested briefly there before going on to join the main army. In August nine regiments of New Jersey militia were drawn from the camp to work on the fortifications of Fort Lee and patrol the Palisades.

On July 18, when General Mercer chanced to have some transient Continental regiments available to stiffen his command, he led a raid against the Hessians on Staten Island. But adverse wind and tide, which were followed by a gale, made the crossing from Thompson's Creek impossible. A second attempt, on October 17, yielded a few British and Hessian prisoners. In general, however, duty in the Flying Camp was a sore trial of patience. The militiamen, bored by the deadly round of military ritual, homesick, and anxious about their crops as harvest time drew near and passed, became a growing nuisance to the communities into which they were crowded. Inadequately supplied in every respect, they wrecked fences for firewood and stripped cornfields to supplement their scanty and uncertain rations. The shortage of powder and bullets was discouraging: a collection of window weights to supply lead for bullets was made in several towns. Malingering became frequent, and plain desertion only less so as July dragged into August. After that the news that came across the Hudson turned their boredom into profound discouragement.

It was July 3 when Howe's force arrived at the Narrows. Not until August 1 did Sir Henry Clinton and Lord Cornwallis join him with the expeditionary force that the guns of Fort Sullivan had repulsed at Charleston, South Carolina, at the end of June. But on August 12

Admiral Lord Howe's fleet of thirty warships convoying four hundred transports that were laden with Hessians and a brigade of the Guards brought his brother Sir William Howe's troops up to thirty-two thousand men. It was the largest expedition that England had ever sent abroad.

To face it Washington had 20,238 men fit for duty in his Continental and militia regiments. But he had to distribute them in his defenses all the way from Kingsbridge, on the Harlem River, to Brooklyn, for the British warships were quick to demonstrate their ability to go where they would, regardless of the fire of American batteries; and there was, of course, no comparison in organization, discipline, and equipment between his hastily levied troops and the professional British and Hessian battalions about to attack them.

Near the end of August General Howe ferried his troops over to Long Island and on the twenty-seventh routed the brigades of Lord Stirling and General John Sullivan, making prisoners of both generals and more than a thousand of their officers and men. Thanks to night and fog and the skill of Colonel John Glover's regiment of Marblehead fishermen, the rest of the American troops were successfully ferried over to New York. But on September 15 the city was evacuated by a retreat which, under the fire of the British warships off Kipp's Bay, became what Washington called "disgraceful and dastardly."

At Harlem Heights next day, to be sure, the American troops, their morale miraculously recovered, turned on their pursuers and threw them back, fighting in the open field at forty yards. But when Washington fortified the naturally strong position between the Hudson and the Harlem, Howe landed his troops at Pell's Point on Long Island Sound and by an advance through Westchester that threatened Washington's line of communica-

Surprise Landing of Cornwallis' Troops

The landing took place at the Fort of the Palisades, November 20, 1776. From a contemporary drawing by a British engineer, probably Lord Rawdon.

Water Color from Emmett Collection, New York Public Library

tions forced him to retire to White Plains. There he fought a successful defensive battle on October 28. Then Howe assembled a force of twenty thousand to attack his thirteen thousand, and Washington could only retire again and on the night of November 1 take up a strong position on the heights of North Castle, five miles farther up the river.

Only Fort Washington and Fort Lee now stood in the way of an invasion of New Jersey and a British advance on Philadelphia: the battery at Paulus Hook had been evacuated some weeks before. The uselessness of Fort Washington had been demonstrated on November 5 when British warships and transports had smashed through the obstructions between the two forts, giving Howe, whose position now lay between Fort Washington and the American army, a direct line of supply from New York. Washington and a council of war decided that the fort should be evacuated, but repeated resolutions by Congress had urged that it be held at all costs.

On the eighteenth, however, it fell to an assault by overwhelming numbers, while Washington on the ramparts of Fort Lee shed tears of helpless rage and pity at the sight of the Hessians bayoneting defenders who had thrown down their arms. Three days later Cornwallis crossed the Hudson at Yonkers, and a Bergen County Tory, Major John Aldington, led him, at the head of twelve British regiments, by a precipitous path up the Palisades at Closter in a movement against the rear of General Nathanael Greene's position at Fort Lee. So swift and secret was the march of the British that only the late warning of a Patriot farmer and a helter-skelter retreat enabled Greene's force to reach a precarious refuge behind the Hackensack River. The invasion of New Jersey had begun.

At the village of Hackensack, Washington, with a force of 5000 men that he had brought down from North Castle by a circuitous march of sixty-five miles, united Greene's command with his own and began that dreary retreat that was to touch the low-water mark of Patriot fortunes for the entire war. The loss of the two forts had cost him invaluable artillery, equipment and supplies, and about 3000 of his best troops, of whom 2800 were prisoners. The weather was execrable, bitterly chill, with fog and heavy rains. Much of the tentage had been lost or abandoned for want of transportation; and many of Greene's men had lost even their blankets, so hasty had been their retreat.

Cornwallis kept in close pursuit; his men, flushed with their recent success, marched twenty miles a day on the mud roads of the time, though their packs and equipment weighed a hundred pounds. Washington hoped to make a stand against them at Newark, even to drive them back. But his troops were too few to hold the line of the Passaic; those left in the Flying Camp had simply drifted away, and he had no entrenching tools. At New Brunswick the British and American artillery cannonaded each other across the Raritan. The Americans partially destroyed the bridge. But now the Maryland and New Jersey militia went home, their terms of enlistment having expired; desertion became epidemic among the rest; and no new regiments arrived in answer to the Legislature's call for men to serve a mere six weeks with the Continental army. So, after burning the military supplies that had been collected at the town and the remaining tentage, since he lacked wagons and horses to remove it, Washington could only continue his retreat.

In their bivouacs the men slept in circles on the ground, with their feet toward the fires. Their clothes were in rags, shoes worn out: the regulation buff and blue of their uniforms rapidly becoming, one humorist observed, "all buff." The Commander in Chief fared little better than his men, he and his staff sleeping more than one night in the open and dining, as he wrote, "on little better than stinking whisky (and not always that) and a bit of beef without vegetables." "We never sup," wrote one of his aides.

Had Howe not sent Cornwallis orders to halt his pursuit until Howe should join him, it seems Washington's army must have been destroyed. That delay gave Washington a week that was invaluable. He detached some of his few remaining troops to put down a Tory uprising in Monmouth County, left Lord Stirling, who, like Sullivan, had been exchanged after the battle on Long Island, to make a stand at Princeton with the Delaware regiment and the five Virginia regiments in case of need, and led the rest on to Trenton.

There he collected boats to take his army across the river and had the left bank scoured for miles up and down so that none should be left in which the enemy could follow him. Back at Princeton a day or two later, he rode with the rear guard of Stirling's command, directing the felling of trees across the highway to delay the British pursuit, and on Sunday, December 8, he saw the last of his troops across the river, as the British, with bands blaring and colors flying, marched into the town behind him.

One of Howe's officers, angry at the leisurely conduct of the pursuit observed that Sir William had calculated with the greatest nicety the exact time needed by the enemy to escape. A salvo from a battery on the opposite shore greeted the appearance of the General and his staff on the Trenton bank, splashed him with mud, and broke a leg of the horse of one of his aides.

Cornwallis promptly led a strong force up the river and occupied Pennington—Penny Town to him and to Washington as well—but search as he would, not one boat could be found. And a search downstream was equally fruitless.

So Washington's army was saved—at least until the river should freeze hard enough to bear the weight of artillery, which was likely to happen on any one of these bitter December nights. But that army numbered only a little more than three thousand men now, and half of these would be free to go home on the expiration of their enlistments at the end of the month. The front they had to guard—from the present site of New Hope to a point below Bristol—was thirty miles long. Only a few regiments now numbered as many as two hundred present and fit for duty. Some were down to between forty and ninety men. Pneumonia and dysentery were rife among them; typhus made its dread appearance. His "little handful," Washington wrote, was "daily decreasing."

Thomas Paine, whose *Common Sense* had set the Colonies flaming with revolutionary spirit the previous January, had ridden with General Greene as a volunteer aide throughout the retreat. Huddled by the bivouac fires he had been busy with another such trumpet note, the first of a series that he was to call *The Crisis*. "These are the times to try men's souls," were its opening words; and surely few men's souls have been more sorely tried than Washington's in these December days.

"You can form no idea of the perplexity of my situation," Washington wrote to his brother. "No man, I believe, ever had a greater choice of difficulties or less means to extricate himself from them. . . . The game," he continued, was "pretty nearly up" unless every nerve was strained to create a new army. And to his adjutant general, Colonel Joseph Reed, whose duties had called him down the river, he wrote: "Necessity, dire necessity will, nay, must, justify my attack."

For there was still no prospect of the arrival of the new regiments the various states were tardily raising, and to keep his troops where they were meant that cold, nakedness, disease, and despair would destroy them, as Howe evidently expected that they would. Ten days after Washington had crossed the river Howe had ordered his troops into winter quarters. He had sent Sir Henry Clinton, with six thousand men, to capture Newport in Rhode Island, and had himself gone back to the delights of his mistress and the pleasures of the gaming table in New York. Cornwallis, confident that Washington was definitely eliminated, had put his luggage on board ship to return to England and an ailing wife.

As the December days had gone by, however, the forces under Washington's immediate command had been strengthened, at least temporarily. Three battalions of militia from Philadelphia, citizens who called themselves "Associators," had joined him under the command of General John Cadwalader; and with them had come Captain Thomas Forrest's battery and Captain Samuel Morris' troop of light horse, a godsend to a commander who had thus far suffered grievously from a total want of cavalry. These numbered about a thousand men in all, and to them were added a regiment of Pennsylvania and Maryland Germans and some small detachments of New Jersey militia from Hunterdon and Middlesex counties. Fresh from home, all of them were well clothed and well shod. Collections of old clothes and shoes were made in Philadelphia and other cities and towns in a vain effort to meet the needs of the Continental troops. But all the men were now well fed from wagon trains organized by patriotic Philadelphia citizens and were still, as Thomas Paine had written of them during the retreat, "defeated but not beaten."

To reunite the forces which Howe's successes on the Hudson had forced him to divide Washington had given orders to General Charles Lee at North Castle and to General William Heath in the Highland passes to march at once to join him. General Philip Schuyler at Albany had responded to his call for help by sending him seven battalions. But Lee, who evidently looked to Washington's final defeat as the means of his obtaining the chief command of the Continental forces, did all he could to delay the march of these troops until an enterprising party of British dragoons captured him in his nightshirt near Basking Ridge on December 12. Not until December 20 did his troops, under Sullivan's command, and the Schuyler battalions led by Benedict Arnold, reach Washington. With Cornwallis on the direct road, they had been compelled to march by way of Morristown, Pittstown, and Easton. Hardship and fatigue had reduced their numbers to about two thousand. They were described as "wanting everything." But their arrival put Washington in command of a total of about six thousand men.

Opposite him, to be sure, at Trenton and in the Bordentown country lay two Hessian brigades that were considered to be among the finest troops in Europe; a British brigade occupied Princeton; and two brigades of Guards were at New Brunswick. But the intervals between these posts were too great for them to be able to support each other properly. "Now is the time to clip their wings while they are so spread," was Washington's comment on the situation as his excellent secret service reported it to him.

From a council of war on Christmas Eve orders were sent down to Cadwalader at Bristol to cross the river with his Associators and a New England brigade on Christmas night and engage the Hessians around Bordentown. A thousand Pennsylvania and New Jersey militia were given orders to cross opposite Trenton that same night and seize the bridge over the Assunpink at the lower end of the town, thus cutting off the retreat of the Hessians in that direction, while Washington led a picked force of 2400 men, with 18 guns, against them at the upper end by a night march from McConkey's ferry down the left back of the Delaware.

The troops assembled in the early twilight of Christmas Day, with their blankets and three-days cooked rations, fresh flints for their muskets, and 40 rounds of ammunition per man. Though their broken shoes and rag-bound feet left bloody tracks in the snow, their hearts were high. Paine's *Crisis,* hurriedly printed in Philadelphia and rushed to the army, had been read to every corporal's guard. "Victory or Death" was the password. The Marblehead men brought the boats out of their concealment behind Malta Island, loaded the men and guns on board, and amid sleet and snow that was driven by a fierce northeast wind pushed off into the river that swirled amid cakes of floating ice.

Big flatboats of shallow draft that were ordinarily used to bring iron ore down from the upper river, Durham boats were admirably suited for the transport of the field guns, their teams and the horses of the mounted officers and the Philadelphia Light Horse. The men of nearby Hopewell, bitter at the treatment they and their families had received from British and Hessians alike, flocked down to the shore to help in the debarkation. Once ashore the whole force marched to the village of Birmingham and there divided, Sullivan, with the right wing and three batteries of artillery, taking the river road, while Greene, with Washington riding beside him, led the left wing, the rest of the guns, and the light horse down the Pennington road. The two wings were to attack simultaneously "one hour before day," according to orders. But there had been maddening delays. It was broad daylight when they came in sight of the Hessian outposts at the northern end of Trenton.

II

"NOT THE WORST GENERAL"

W‌ASHINGTON'S PLAN that December night aimed at far
more than the capture of Trenton. If all should go well
there, it might be so extended as to bring about a complete reversal of the strategic situation. Not only did
the enemy's dispositions favor such an outcome: a change
that had occurred in the attitude of the Jersey people in
the past fortnight invited it.

General Sir William Howe had striven to make submission as easy as possible for the people of the con-
quered Jerseys. In September, endowed by the Crown
with the powers of Peace Commissioners, he and his
brother Admiral Howe had proclaimed that the King
was "most graciously disposed to direct a revision of
such of his Royal Instructions as may be construed to
lay an improper Restraint upon the Freedom of Legisla-
tion in any of his Colonies, and to concur in the revisal
of all Acts by which His Subjects may think themselves
agrieved."

On November 30, with the Jerseys—or at least that
part of them that counted strategically—under his control, the General had joined the Admiral in proclaiming
that although "several Bodies of armed men . . . do
still continue their opposition," a full pardon, with the
assurance of liberty and the enjoyment of their property,
would be granted to all who, within sixty days, would

swear to "remain in a peaceful Obedience to His Majesty and not take up arms, or encourage others to take up arms, in Opposition to His Authority."

As Howe's army advanced and finally went into winter quarters on a line running from Perth Amboy through New Brunswick and Princeton to Trenton and down the Delaware to Burlington, more and more people hastened to sign this oath, which could be administered by any British officer. There was much to excuse their doing so, especially the sight of Washington's depleted army, ragged and ill shod, tramping southward through the mud, without making more than the semblance of a stand against its pursuers. At Newark, when Washington withdrew his flanking troops from Elizabeth Town and Perth Amboy, panic had seized the populace: the strictest Presbyterians had ignored the observance of the Sabbath in their efforts to hide their goods from the approaching invaders. At Princeton the Reverend Doctor Witherspoon, having dismissed the students of the College of New Jersey in "a very affectionate manner," had departed on horseback at the side of his wife, who rode in the family chaise.

The Legislature, which had been sitting at Princeton and on the day of the Battle of Long Island had elected William Livingston governor, had adjourned to Trenton, and thence to Burlington, where it soon broke up. The State government virtually ceased to exist, its more prominent members going into hiding. John Hart, its Speaker, returned to his home at Hopewell to find the village ravaged by the enemy, his wife dead, and his children refugees in the Sourland Mountains.

As the British approached Princeton, Richard Stockton, who had lately returned from inspecting the deplorably ill-clothed New Jersey troops in the Ticonderoga country, escaped with his family to the house of a friend in Monmouth County, only to be captured by the Tories and treated by the British with special severity as a signer of the Declaration of Independence. Other conspicuous Patriots had crowded the ferry houses on the Delaware in search of safety in Pennsylvania's Bucks County, and farther south and west. The news from outside the area occupied by the British was devastating. The Continental Congress, after directing that Philadelphia be defended to the last, had decamped to the safety of Baltimore; and news of General Lee's capture was a great blow, for many believed him to be a better general than Washington.

So it is hardly to be wondered at if, as Howe maintained, some twenty-seven hundred of New Jersey's citizens—and among them members of the Assembly and certain officials of the state government—sought the King's pardon and renewed their allegiance to the Crown. In return they received what was called a "protection paper," that was supposed to secure them, their persons, families, and property, from oppression and depredation by the troops under Howe's command; and Howe, true to his policy of conciliation, had repeatedly issued orders to make sure that these papers were respected.

Nevertheless, his troops had fallen upon the New Jersey people "tooth and claw." To the British soldiers the Americans were rebels; the rebellion of "the Forty-five" with "Bloody Cumberland's" suppression of it, was recent enough to be well remembered. The discipline of the British regiments, moreover, had suffered through the enlistment of recruits of a low order—the war was so unpopular in England that enough good men could not be had; and there were often no more than two officers to a company. To the Hessians the Americans were scum, peasants—*canaille* to the Hessian officers— fighting for "Liberty," an incomprehensible word to them. The British soldiery laughed at the "protection papers." For the Hessians, of course, they might just as well have been written in Greek.

The plundering of the towns, villages, and farmhouses by the men of the baggage trains became commonplace. At Elizabeth Town their doxies stood guard over the growing heaps of loot. The Hessians had been told that service in America would give them the opportunity to make their fortunes. Not content with sacking a village, they left its dwellings—notably at Hopewell and Maidenhead (now Lawrenceville)—with smashed windows and doors torn from their hinges. The behavior of the British, as Washington appears to have gathered from reports, was even worse. It was said that when one of their generals shifted his billet he took with him the furniture that he liked in his former quarters.

At Princeton not only were the homes of such leading Patriots as John Witherspoon, Richard Stockton, and Jonathan Sergeant sacked, pictures slashed, and libraries destroyed, but, although General Alexander Leslie had his headquarters in the village and the garrison was composed of English troops, Nassau Hall was also pillaged. The contents of its library and museum, its scientific and mathematical instruments, and the "celebrated orrery," said to be the finest planetarium in the world, were scattered or destroyed. Two grist mills and a fulling mill nearby were burned wantonly together with their contents. Milch cows were stolen at night and slaughtered with other cattle; orchards were chopped down for firewood. It was said that General James Grant together with Cornwallis and Leslie had stood by while horses and hogs were driven off without any compensation being made for them. At best only a receipt—hardly ever any money—was given on even the most formal requisition.

Worse still, inevitably, human nature being what it is, the ugly word, rape, began to be whispered about. At nearby Penn's Neck a farm girl was strangled and ravished by two British light horsemen; an outraged father was killed when he shot a British officer who attempted to violate his daughter; and several women and girls were suspected of suffering in silence rather than endure the shame involved in bringing accusations against soldiers who had assaulted them.

It became the turn of the Tories to range the country in armed bands, plundering Patriot farms as the Patriots had plundered theirs. Informers who supplied British headquarters with the names of men serving in the American army were rewarded with goods confiscated from the homes of their victims. Estates were held forfeited on the word of an informer. Slaves were rewarded with their freedom for denouncing their masters. Quakers and Loyalists suffered alike from these abuses. The plundering became so promiscuous that many believed the "protection papers" had been issued only to make sure that those who obtained them would keep their property where the plunderers could easily find it. The Loyalists, who had expected peace and security with the coming of the British, began to distrust Howe and dislike his troops. One of them attacked him bitterly in verse, writing of the "protection papers":

> This magical mantle o'er property thrown
> Secured it from all sorts of thieves but his own.

In Bergen County and on up the Hudson as far as Tappan in New York state the Loyalists were predominant. Their treatment of Patriot neighbors was so outrageous that General William Heath turned aside in his march to join Washington long enough to destroy their supplies at Hackensack and, with the aid of New York militia under General George Clinton, capture a number of men from a newly raised Loyalist battalion near Bergen Woods. Down along the lower Delaware Tories and

Patriots were so evenly matched that they appear to have raided each other, turn and turn about. Up in the hills, with Morristown as their base, Patriot militia, numbering between seven hundred and one thousand men, were soon raiding the lowlands for cattle that would otherwise have gone to feed the enemy.

The road from Princeton to Trenton and down the river to Burlington became increasingly unhealthy for British and Hessian messengers, patrols, and scouting parties. As he rode back to New York, Howe himself was fired on from ambush by a party of five farmers, of whom his escort wounded two and killed one. Guerrilla warfare —something beyond the experience of the Hessians— harassed both Colonel Johann Rall's brigade at Trenton and the brigade which occupied the Bordentown area under Colonel Karl von Donop, the division commander. Night after night their outposts were beaten up; their hundred-man guard at the Crosswicks drawbridge, essential to their communications, was assailed by parties of armed civilians that had neither officers nor military organization.

Burlington, where there were many Loyalists, von Donop dared not occupy, lest Commodore Thomas Seymour, commander of the Pennsylvania squadron that patrolled the river below Trenton, should bombard it. Seymour threw a few round shot into it to support his threat, and von Donop had no guns heavy enough to drive off the Pennsylvania row galleys and gondolas. He established his headquarters at Bordentown, crowded his men into the neighboring farmhouses, from which the inhabitants had fled, taking their bedding with them. He sent the British 42nd Foot, Highlanders who had been attached to his command, as far as Mount Holly to protect the Loyalists thereabouts from a raid by four or five hundred Virginia and some New Jersey militia.

The situation was easier for Colonel Rall up at

Trenton. The town's hundred houses, two churches, Quaker Meeting House, and the barracks built in French and Indian War days, furnished adequate housing for his 1400 veteran troops. With the military snob's contempt for the raw troops he had three times defeated, he neglected to build a redoubt where the Pennington and Princeton roads met the heads of King and Queen Streets (now Warren and Broad Streets), as von Donop had ordered him to do, and he kept his guns parked, one behind another, in the center of the town. But he stationed strong and vigilant outposts at all important places and kept his *jägers* and the twenty troopers of the Bristish 16th Light Dragoons, detailed to his command, on frequent patrols; and one of his three regiments was constantly under arms.

He was annoyed by the increasing frequency with which his outposts and patrols were attacked and his messengers to Princeton captured or killed. He urged upon Major General Sir James Grant, who was in command at New Brunswick, and upon General Alexander Leslie at Princeton, the necessity of placing the wing of a regiment at Maidenhead lest his communications be cut entirely. But Grant, who had boasted in Parliament that he could march from one end of the American continent to the other with five thousand men, refused, with the comment that he could keep the peace in New Jersey with a corporal's guard. Rall send a hundred men and a cannon with his next messenger.

Most of his time went to the enjoyment of the comforts and privileges of his position, gambling and drinking half the night and sleeping till ten in the morning, at which time he rose to loll at his window in his dressing gown and watch the daily parade of his troops in the street below. When Major von Dechow, his second-in-command, urged the building of the fortifications that had been ordered, his reply was: "Let them come. We want no trenches. We will go at them with the bayonet." He called "old woman's talk" the reports that reached him on December 23 that the Americans across the river had been ordered to prepare three-days cooked rations.

It was in vain that Grant sent him a warning, in vain that a skirmish at one of his outposts early in the evening of Christmas Day revealed a confusion that resulted from a complete lack of orders dealing with an attack. Supping jovially at Mr. Abraham Hunt's at King and Second Streets, he thrust into his pocket, unread, a final note of warning that a Pennsylvania farmer left at the door when the butler denied him entrance. He lingered late over cards and wine and went to bed so drunk that his brigade adjutant had to call him twice when the early morning air rang with shouts of *"Der Feind! Der Feind! Heraus! Heraus!"* and the banging of musket shots.

Greene and Sullivan had taken care to synchronize the march of their columns, and their attacks were almost simultaneous. The Hessian outposts, still drowsy, fell back at once, firing as they went. The British Light Dragoons, between whom and their German comrades little love appears to have been lost, had only time to saddle their horses and ride hell-for-leather for Princeton and safety, before two of Greene's brigades swept past the northern entrance to the town and formed a line that closed the gap between the Princeton road and Assunpink Creek. His guns went into action at the junction of King and Queen Streets, the very spot where the redoubt would have been, if Rall had obeyed von Donop's orders. Stirling's brigade formed their support, while Mercer's, swinging to the right, made contact with Sullivan's line and, the priming of their muskets sodden, attacked with bayonet and gun-butt through the western outskirts of the town.

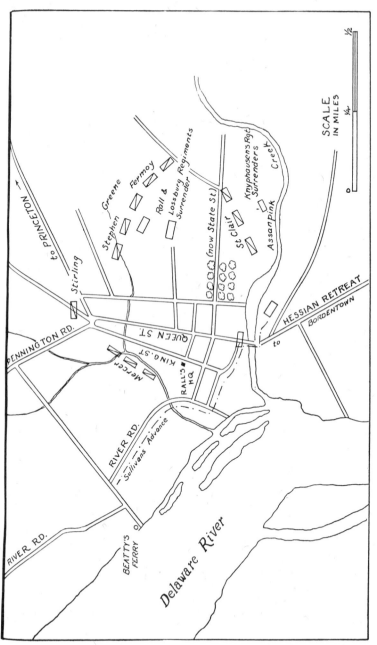

The Battle of Trenton

King Street is now Warren Street, and Queen Street is now Broad Street.
From the author's *The Campaign of Princeton*

Shells from young Alexander Hamilton's battery smashed the vanguard of the Lossberg Regiment as it emerged from Church Alley under orders to clear Queen Street, and the regiment retreated to the eastern edge of the town, where it reformed facing northeast. Rall attempted to lead his own regiment to the attack up King Street. But, met by the fire of Greene's artillery and assailed on its left by Mercer's infantry, his column broke in such disorder that it threw the left wing of the Lossbergs into confusion. Driving through streets befogged by blowing sleet and cannon smoke, half-blocked by plunder-laden wagons, and ringing with cheers and yells and the screams of the wounded, Stirling's men seized the bridge over the Assunpink, though not before some six hundred fugitives had made good their escape across it, and pushed the Knyphausen regiment out Second Street into the marshy country several hundred yards up the stream.

Rallying some remnants of his own regiment, Rall re-formed them with the Lossbergs and was leading both, with the band playing and colors displayed, in an effort to retake the town, when he fell from his horse, mortally wounded. His troops, faced by Greene's fresh brigades that blocked their last hope of escape, surrendered after a brief parley. About a quarter of a mile to the south of them, the Knyphausen regiment, their commander, von Dechow, also mortally wounded, did the same, and the battle was won.

Just an hour and forty-five minutes had passed since the firing of the first shot. The losses were amazingly small: of the Hessians 106, including Rall and von Dechow, who died of their wounds; of the Americans, none killed and only four wounded, two of whom were enlisted men and the other two Captain William Washington, and eighteen-year-old Lieutenant James Monroe, who was to live to become president of the United

States. But, in the words of a present-day British historian, "it may be doubted whether so small a number of men every employed so short a space of time with greater and more lasting results upon the history of the world."

The roster of officers in the victorious army is rich in names notable in American history. In addition to the Revolutionary heroes: Washington, Greene, Sullivan, Stirling, Mercer, Henry Knox, Glover of the Marblehead fishermen, and Hand of the Pennsylvania riflemen, it includes James Monroe, Alexander Hamilton, Thomas Marshall, whose son was to be the first chief justice of the United States, Richard Clough Anderson, the father of the commander of Fort Sumter in 1861, William Hull, who was to surrender Detroit to the British in 1812, and James Wilkinson of doubtful reputation.

The captured Hessians numbered more than eight hundred. A thousand fine muskets, six excellent field guns, forty horses, wagons, twelve drums and a full set of band instruments were captured. Forty hogsheads of rum were also among the spoils and before Washington's order for their destruction could be carried out, the effect of their contents on the victorious soldiery became disquietingly noticeable.

As soon as he could assemble his principal officers Washington held a council of war to decide on his next move. Greene and Knox, the best read in the military art among them, strongly urged that the victory be followed up at once by an advance down the river against von Donop's troops, which were known to be widely scattered. But the guarding and transport across the river of the prisoners, whose number equaled one-third of Washington's force, would leave him with fewer men than von Donop; and the ice packed against the left bank had prevented both James Ewing's militia opposite Trenton and

Cadwalader's troops at Bristol from making the crossings assigned to them.

So, reluctantly, with the storm in their faces now, the army tramped back to McConkey's ferry. The long column of prisoners and booty delayed the march; the ice in the river was more dangerous than it had been before. It was deep night and bitterly cold by the time the last of them was over. By the time they were back in their old quarters all of them had been marching and fighting for 36 hours, some for 50, and some had marched 40 miles. A thousand men, more than two-fifths of the whole command, were reported unfit for duty next morning.

Washington praised his men in General Orders. He had been in many actions, he told them, and had always perceived some misbehavior in some individuals, but in that action he saw none. Next day he received all 23 of the captured officers at his Newtown headquarters in a manner that they found *sehr angenehm,* and he entertained the captured field officers at dinner. They found him courteous and urbane but thought his physiognomy "crafty," which is hardly surprising since he had routed, with his ragged rabble, their splendid regiments. Then he packed them all off to Philadelphia, the officers in post chaises, the enlisted men on foot, to be paraded through the streets with their captured arms and colors, as indubitable evidence of his victory.

Meanwhile astonishing reports of the effect of that victory kept coming in from down the river. Cadwalader had made good his crossing on the afternoon of the day of the battle and, although he had soon heard of Washington's retirement, he had remained on the Jersey side. The reports of fugitives from Rall's troops that they had been defeated by overwhelming numbers had convinced von Donop that his only safe course was to fall back and reassemble his widely distributed forces at Allentown. Cadwalader had promptly occupied Burlington and Crosswicks, and his mounted patrols were ranging the country to within a few miles of Princeton. Mercer and sixteen hundred Pennsylvania militia were at Bordentown.

Something like consternation had, indeed, prevailed among the British: so sure had they been of their conquest of New Jersey. Word of the defeat at Trenton was brought to Princeton by the flying dragoons, and some fifty officers and men of the Knyphausen regiment who had escaped capture by swimming the Assunpink confirmed it. But Grant at New Brunswick was furious at von Donop's report of his withdrawal to Allentown and ordered him to remain there. Upon a report, however, that fourteen hundred rebels were marching by way of Pennington to join the Jersey militia at Rocky Hill for an attack on Princeton, Leslie ordered von Donop to join him there.

The enemy seemed suddenly to be roving the country at will. A belated detachment of von Donop's force suffered defeat, with the loss of an officer and their guidon, in its march from Allentown. A British baggage train and a patrol of dragoons were captured by a party of American light horse within a few miles of Leslie's outposts. Grant ordered up an additional battalion of Hessians from Perth Amboy; Leslie began to build redoubts at Princeton and occupied Rocky Hill, Kingston, and Maidenhead in force.

But on New Year's Day Grant, leaving only six hundred men at New Brunswick to guard his stores and a military chest of seventy thousand pounds joined Leslie and von Donop with the rest of his troops. That same day Cornwallis, compelled to defer his trip home, rode the fifty miles from New York, assumed command, and next morning, with a force of about eight thousand men and 28 guns including several twelve-pounders, took the road for Trenton. For Washington was again across the river at Trenton and appeared to be waiting for the British to attack him there.

It was again a move dictated by necessity, as Washington saw it. The British were concentrating. How many Continentals would remain with the colors after the expiration of their enlistments on December 31 was highly questionable. "A body of firm troops, inured to danger," as Washington wrote to the President of Congress a few days later, was absolutely necessary to lead the more raw and undisciplined, and to retreat again would be "destroying every dawn of hope which had begun to revive in the hearts of the New Jersey militia."

Vested with the powers of a military dictator by an act of Congress on the twenty-seventh he had his Continentals parade at Trenton and promised them a bounty of ten dollars for another six weeks of service, pledging his private fortune for its payment. Some fourteen or fifteen hundred of them, looking like a flock of "animated scarecrows," according to one observer, "poised their firelocks" to signify their willingness to remain; an almost equal number of Hitchcock's New Englanders did the same; and on New Year's night John Cadwalader's and Thomas Mifflin's men, by a magnificent night march through knee-deep mud, joined them and brought his numbers up to about fifty-two hundred men with some forty guns.

His secret service had kept him well informed of the enemy's movements and evident intentions. Throughout the thirty-first and New Year's Day he had kept all his available men busy at fortifying the commanding eastern bank of the Assunpink, and on the morning of January 2, 1777, he sent Hand's riflemen, the German battalion, a regiment of Virginia Continentals and Forrest's battery up the Princeton road to meet Cornwallis' column and delay its advance as much as possible. This they did with such a will that the British, who were moreover hampered by the deep mud, took ten hours for the ten-mile march. The early winter twilight had begun to fall when, after a sharp fight at the edge of the town, the last of the Virginians made good their retreat across the bridge over the Assunpink, under cover of the fire of the American guns and infantry on the ridge above them.

What followed was the seldom noticed Second Battle of Trenton. Washington called it "a cannonade." Knox made light of it. The American losses were small; those of the British were never published. But they have been estimated at some five hundred killed and wounded. Three stubborn attacks on the bridge by the British infantry, and one at a ford lower down the stream, were driven back by the small-arms fire of the entrenched Americans before Cornwallis decided to give his weary troops a night's rest and "bag the fox" in the morning. He saw Washington trapped, with the flowing river on his left, wide-open country on his right flank, and only the single road down the river to Bordentown open to his retreat. The American watch fires burned brightly all night long. But daybreak showed the trenches empty, and with sunrise came from far to the north the sound of volleys of musketry and the boom of cannon. "The fox" had "stolen away."

Washington had held a council of war at eleven o'clock that night, and an hour or so later the leading elements of his army were marching for Princeton by a route the existence of which, according to various legends, was dramatically made known to him only at the last moment. Actually, his adjutant general had been having it patrolled since the previous day. It is, moreover, hardly conceivable that a general of Washington's experience and sagacity—and as well acquainted with the country as he was—should have placed his army in a trap and kept it there a whole day, without knowing how he was to extricate it.

Beginning with "the Sand Town road," the present-day Hamilton Avenue, his route ran northeasterly over the Barrens and past Bear Swamp to meet the Quaker Road, which led to the Stony Brook Meeting House and thence, a couple of miles farther on, to Princeton. His hope was to surprise and rout the British garrison there before daylight and then, if Providence continued to favor him, to press on to New Brunswick and its store of supplies and British gold.

The march went well. The temperature had dropped sharply during the afternoon and evening, congealing the mud of the roads. The guns bumped briskly over the frozen ruts; the men, though many of them had marched the whole of the previous night or fought more than half of the previous day, tramped doggedly on—and fell asleep on their feet at every halt. But day had dawned clear and cold by the time the head of the column reached the Stony Brook Meeting House.

There, while the main column proceeded toward Princeton, Mercer's brigade was detached to delay the British pursuit by seizing and destroying the bridge that carried the post road over Stony Brook, about a mile to the north, where U.S. Route 206 crosses the brook to-day. Within a few minutes, however, a column of enemy infantry was sighted on the post road, already over the bridge and marching toward Trenton. It was the British 17th Foot, part of the Fourth Brigade, which Cornwallis had left at Princeton with orders for the 17th and the 55th Regiments to follow him next day. At sight of the strong American column marching toward Princeton, Colonel Charles Mawhood, the brigade commander, promptly turned back to join his other regiments in de-fense of the village. Informed by his scouts of the pres-

ence of Mercer's force, which by this time was retiring across country to rejoin the main column, Mawhood left the road and moved to attack it.

The fight that followed was brief and bloody. The volleys of the weary Americans did little damage. The fresh British troops charged and swept Mercer's men before them. Mercer, unhorsed and fighting sword in hand, fell mortally wounded by seven bayonet thrusts. His routed command, streaming to the rear, threw into disorder and panic the Pennsylvanians, whom Greene was hurrying from the main column to support them. But Moulder's battery on the crest near the Thomas Clark house opened on the pursuers with grapeshot. Within a few minutes Washington, who had been riding at the head of the main column, had galloped back and rallied the Pennsylvanians. The 7th Virginia and Hand's riflemen assailed Mawhood's left flank and the column's rear guard, the veteran New Englanders, his right.

Although now greatly outnumbered and attacked in front and on both flanks, Mawhood's men formed line and opened fire and, though they broke under the grapeshot of the American guns, formed again. They finally broke and, leaving almost a quarter of their number dead or wounded on the field, fled helter-skelter for the post road and the bridge, with Hand's riflemen racing after them and Washington galloping with the pursuers and shouting: "It's a fine fox chase, my boys!"

Generals Arthur St. Clair and Sullivan with the advance section of the American column now moved forward against the remainder of the Fourth Brigade, the

Washington at the Close of the Battle of Princeton

General Mercer is mortally wounded. Nassau Hall appears in the background.

From the painting by Charles Wilson Peale
Courtesy of Princeton University

BATTLE of PRINCETON

SCALE
IN YARDS

500   0   500

LEGEND

AMERICAN

BRITISH

Post Road

to TRENTON

Maivhood when
first seen by
Americans

WORTH'S MILL

Stony Brook

Route of Mercer Rd

Route of

Washington's Main Army

Quakers

T. CLARK

QUAKER MEETING HOUSE

MAWHOOD vs
WASHINGTON

W. CLARK'S
ORCHARD

MAWHOOD v.
MERCER

55th Rgt

(present Mercer Rd)

ST. CLAIR

SULLIVAN

FROG

HOLLOW

Back Rd

55th Rgt

40th Rgt

REDOUBT

NASSAU HALL

to KINGSTON →

The Battle of Princeton

From the author's *The Campaign of Princeton*

40th and 55th Regiments, which had formed on a ridge near the southeast edge of the village. But, shaken by the knowledge of Mawhood's defeat, they were quickly routed by a surprise attack on their flank and fled, most of them down the Rocky Hill road (now Witherspoon Street) and a few to the refuge of Nassau Hall, where solid shot from Alexander Hamilton's guns quickly produced their surrender.

A crack British brigade had been annihilated. Some three hundred men, all told, were made prisoners. Washington estimated the British dead at about one hundred, and Howe admitted a total loss of 265. The American losses were only 30 enlisted men and four officers, but among them were some of the best and the bravest: able and experienced officers, of whom the American army had only too few. General Mercer died of his wounds after nine days of lingering agony. The wounded were established in emergency hospitals in the village and in the two Clark farmhouses on the battlefield, where the eminent Philadelphia surgeon, Doctor Benjamin Rush, was soon in attendance upon them.

Among the spoils of victory were the two fine brass fieldpieces of the vanquished brigade, the blankets—invaluable to the destitute Americans—which the British soldiers had discarded along with their packs upon going into action, a considerable quantity of supplies, about a hundred oxen, some sheep, and a number of fine horses. Collection of all these and arrangements for their transport and the burning of the enemy's store of hay and grain had taken about two hours when the sound of brisk firing at the bridge over Stony Brook indicated that Leslie's brigade, which Cornwallis had left at Maidenhead was engaged in a sharp fight with the party of Pennsylvania militia which had been sent to destroy the bridge.

Cornwallis, with his whole force, soon joined Leslie,

and the Pennsylvanians were forced to retire, leaving their task only half completed. But Cornwallis, suspecting an ambush on the tortuous road beyond the brook, made an elaborate reconnaissance before advancing to the village; and by that time Washington's army, with its column of prisoners, captured stores and cattle, was nearing Kingston on the road to New Brunswick.

A brisk rear-guard action against the pursuing light troops of the enemy gave the Americans ample time to destroy the bridge at Kingston. But there Washington wheeled to his left and took the road to Morristown. For with Cornwallis so close on his heels, the tempting military stores and treasure at New Brunswick were beyond the reach of even his long-enduring soldiers. They slept that night at Somerset Court House (now Millstone), at Pluckemin the next, and on January 6 reached Morristown.

Cornwallis, meanwhile, desperately anxious about the safety of the stores and the military chest, had marched straight on through the night to New Brunswick, where at dawn he found the slender garrison drawn up on the heights to receive the American attack and the treasure and much of the stores in the safety of the farther bank of the Raritan River. The campaign was over, in his opinion and in that of General Howe: next summer would be soon enough to begin another. The British forces in the Jerseys were crowded into winter quarters at Perth Amboy and New Brunswick, with the Raritan as a safe line of communications and supply. But the Jersey people now appeared to be quite different from the despairing population that the British believed they had subjugated four weeks ago, and at Morristown Washington was building high hopes of demonstrating that fact.

III

A MILITARY GAME OF CHESS

In London, where the government had proclaimed the occupation of Newport as practically bringing the war to an end, the news of the Trenton-Princeton campaign and its consequences were more frankly accepted than they were in British headquarters in New York where an atmosphere of wishful thinking prevailed. Horace Walpole, who had come to believe that nothing but the armed intervention of France could save the American cause, commented drily that the campaign had "lost much of its florid complexion, and General Washington is allowed by both sides not to be the worst general in the field."

As the days went by, General Howe himself was moved to inform Lord George Germain, Secretary of State for the Colonies, "with much concern" that the enemy's successes had "thrown us further back than was at first apprehended, from the great encouragement it has given the rebels." Of New Jersey a British officer wrote, doubtless with some exaggeration: "the revolt all at once became universal." Actually, however, the Jersey militia had forced the British to evacuate their posts at Hackensack, Newark, and Elizabeth Town, and the ten thousand troops that occupied Perth Amboy and New Brunswick, with strong detachments at Raritan Landing and Bonhamtown, dominated little territory beyond the range of their muskets.

At Washington's orders the militia swept the sur-

rounding country clean of supplies and of the wagons and horses to haul them. The British foraging expeditions were so heavily assailed by parties of wily farmers that they had to be escorted by not less than two battalions. Supplies had to be brought from New York to meet the shortages in food, fodder, and fuel, and the boats that supplied the posts up the Raritan were pestered by sharpshooters on the banks, and one was sunk by cannon shot at the Roundabouts. Many horses died for want of forage. Continual raids on the outposts made the nights hideous, and by day the men were kept busy building redoubts and entrenchments. Crowded into inadequate billets in the little towns, many of them fell sick. Smallpox broke out. The militiamen, with their knowledge of the country and burning with the animosity with which the British occupation and Tory persecution had filled them, were the best possible troops for making the enemy garrisons miserable. For example, on January 20 they, with a stiffening of Pennsylvania riflemen, routed a British raid on the flour mills at Millstone, capturing forty wagons and a hundred of the enemy's precious horses.

Up in the hills at Morristown, as the bleak weeks of January went by, Washington could congratulate himself that, although a lack of sufficient regulars had prevented his resuming the offensive as he had hoped to do, he had not been compelled to retire to Pennsylvania, with his army dribbling away on the march, as Howe had expected it would. He was, moreover, admirably situated

The Ford Mansion at Morristown

Washington's famous headquarters has been well restored and preserved by the National Park Service.

Courtesy of National Park Service, Morristown National Historical Park, Morristown, New Jersey

both strategically and tactically for the renewal of active warfare when fresh troops did arrive.

With an adequate force at Princeton under the command of General Israel Putnam, who was strengthening the fortifications that the British had built there, and with General Heath in command of the forts at Peekskill, he controlled the absolutely essential line of communications between New England and the central and southern states: Wayne in the fortress at Ticonderoga blocked the invasion route from Canada. Couriers from Congress, which had lost no time in returning to Philadelphia, could reach him at Morristown by less than a day and night of hard riding. When the new campaign opened, he would be on the enemy's flank if Howe again advanced on Philadelphia, as seemed most likely, and if Howe moved to attack the forts on the Hudson, a few rapid marches would bring Washington's army to their support.

Tactically the Morristown position was equally advantageous. A blockhouse and entrenchments fortified an advance post with Greene's division supporting it at Basking Ridge. The main body of the army was established in the Loantaka Valley some three miles from the village green. Steep slopes and deep ravines afforded excellent defensive positions for front and flanks. A Liberty Tree stood in the center of the camp. The tents of the officers lined a well-graded main street 80 feet wide, which was used as a parade ground. On streets parallel to it the soldiers built their huts in blocks of four or five together, which were neither too uncomfortable nor too unsanitary by the standards of the time. The surrounding country was rich in provender and forage. There were log storehouses and cabins for the commissaries and sutlers, and the local population was strong in its support of the Patriot cause.

Morristown itself was described by the wife of a Virginia colonel of light horse as "a clever little village." There were some fifty dwellings, two churches—Presbyterian and Baptist—and two taverns. In one of the latter, Freeman's, Washington established his headquarters in two rooms above the barroom, and in those cramped quarters, until the arrival of his wife early in March, he wrestled with the perplexing and multifarious problems that could be solved only by him, and must be solved if the war was to go on.

The first of these was the need of men. His sanguine plans for resuming active operations after giving his men a brief rest had gone glimmering with the departure of the time-expired Continental regiments and of the Philadelphia militia, who had more than fulfilled their promise of service. If the various states had promptly set about raising the new regiments that Congress had authorized in the past September, he should have had at his disposal many of the seventy-six thousand troops he had been promised. But the three-year enlistment term of Continental service made it unpopular; and each state, concerned for its own safety, was chiefly interested in raising troops for its own defense.

Reinforcements came in so slowly that by the end of January the only regulars remaining at Morristown were 800 Continentals who were slated to go home in another two weeks, five Virginia regiments and three other battalions which the attrition of service had reduced to about one hundred men each. Only the arrival of 700 militia from Massachusetts made it possible to keep up a semblance of strength against an enemy twice as strong. "Oh, that Americans were spirited and resolute!" Greene exclaimed in a letter to his wife. Washington felt himself confronted with a "universal listlessness" and begged Congress to send him every militiaman that Pennsylvania, Maryland, and Virginia could be persuaded to call out. The New Jersey militia, he told Congress, were growing discouraged, exhausted by their continual service against the enemy.

Every officer who could be spared was sent on recruiting duty to fill the many gaps in the existing organizations. The new levies were of poor quality: even a few convicts were discovered among them. And in Greene's opinion many of the officers were inferior to their men in everything but the ability to get themselves elected. Few were conscious of any responsibility for the welfare of their men. Some of those sent on recruiting duty resigned as soon as they reached home. Life in the camp was hard and dull, and the men took to stealing, fighting among themselves, and gambling until Washington stopped it with an order against cards and dice. Their pay was long overdue, but their drinking was only slightly curtailed by the high prices charged by vendors who, to Washington's disgust, swaggered among the huts in the uniforms of colonels and majors of the local militia.

One observer reported that the roads around Morristown were filled with naked and half-starved soldiers. He was doubtless exaggerating. But confusion reigned in the Commissary, for Joseph Trumbull, the able and zealous Commissary General was detained at Philadelphia for the convenience of Congress, and, when Washington made reluctant use of his dictatorial powers and sent out parties to impress provisions locally, the militia frequently plundered what was collected.

In the Quartermaster General's department the disorganization was such that all over the country its subordinates were bidding against each other, and Washington was moved to write personally to the governors of all the states, begging for shoes, shirts, and stockings, the lack of which, he told them, had been the ruin of the old army.

The discipline of the troops, which had never been high, naturally deteriorated under these conditions. In Putnam's command at Princeton a whole company of artillery absconded when the rum ration had run out for several days and Putnam refused to issue all the arrears at once on the arrival of a fresh supply. Desertion became frequent at all the posts. Some men were lured away by British offers of as much as twenty dollars* for a deserter's arms, which appeared in enemy newspapers and were reported in Patriot journals. Others slipped away to enlist as recruits in the new Continental regiments. A man who was willing to risk a hundred lashes of the cat-o'-nine-tails could thus collect the large additional bounty —eighty-six and two-thirds dollars in Massachusetts— which various states were offering.

But sickness was a more serious menace. Smallpox broke out in both camp and village. Vaccination had yet to be discovered, and inoculation, the only known protection, so often caused death that it had been prohibited in Virginia. Washington, however, was a firm believer in its efficacy. He ordered the whole army to be subjected to it and the new troops to be inoculated at the various mobilization centers before joining his command. The spread of the disease was soon checked, and it was eventually eradicated from the army.

But in the meanwhile both the village churches had become crowded hospitals, their congregations cheerfully braving the winter's cold at Sabbath services held out-of-doors. In mid-February when several Hessian battalions and a number of heavy guns from Clinton's command at Newport arrived at Perth Amboy, and Howe's appearance there suggested that he might be about to advance on Philadelphia, Washington had only four thousand men under his immediate command; a thousand of these were in the hospitals; and the New England militia were due to go home in the middle of March. It was with eloquent restraint that he wrote to John Han-

* Dollars: the Spanish silver coin that was current in the Caribbean and circulated widely in the English North American colonies.

cock on March 14 that unless new troops arrived soon, "we must before long expect some interesting and melancholy event."

Early that month Washington himself had come down with an attack of quinsy so severe that cupping was resorted to. But gaps in the dates of his voluminous correspondence indicate that he was not incapacitated for more than a day or two. His recovery was doubtless hastened by the arrival of his wife, who liked to boast in later years that she had generally heard the closing guns of every campaign and the opening ones of the next.

"Lady Washington" to her contemporaries, she arrived in "a plain chariot" but with her postilions dressed in liveries of white and scarlet. She promptly moved her husband to quarters better suited to the dignity of his position, but she dressed and bore herself with great simplicity, often referred to him as "the old man," and soon gathered the ladies in and near the village into groups that knitted and sewed for the needy soldiers.

Several families of wealth and distinction had fled to Morristown from New York and the enemy-occupied areas of New Jersey, the Elias Boudinots and John Morton, "the Rebel banker," among them. The wives of a number of general officers and regimental commanders had joined their husbands during the winter. The fine house of Lord Stirling, brother-in-law of Governor Livingston, was close by at Basking Ridge. The Livingston family spent the winter there, although General Greene had made the house his headquarters, and the Livingston girls and "Lady Kitty," Stirling's daughter, did much at "tea-drinking parties" to brighten the evenings for the young officers. There was a commodious room for assemblies at Freeman's Tavern. Young Alexander Hamilton, whom Washington had made one of his aides, presided at the headquarters dinner table and kept the conversation lively. As spring brought fine days and better traveling conditions, the young ladies and their officer friends made up riding parties and even, on occasion, joined Washington on his daily rides to visit the outposts.

He had been unremitting in these excursions from the first, learning the surrounding country by heart and keeping in close touch with his men, whose loyalty to him personally, which he had won by his fairness, sympathetic understanding, and reckless bravery, came close to equaling their devotion to the cause for which they served. One of them wrote years later of one of these cavalcades: "the brilliant troop of cavaliers . . . their dark blue uniforms with buff facings and glittering military appendages, their cocked hats worn sidelong, with the union cockade . . . all gallantly mounted, tall and graceful, but one towered above the rest. I doubted not an instant that I saw the beloved hero."

Loving horses and riding as he did, these excursions doubtless did much to enable him to bear with invincible equanimity the burden of incessant anxieties that rested upon him. Even when in March Congress adopted a resolution containing a thinly veiled censure for having accomplished so little in the past winter, he replied only with patient irony. Could he confine the enemy to their present quarters, prevent their getting supplies, and totally subdue them, he wrote, he should be "happy indeed"; but his whole force in New Jersey, as shown by the enclosed return, was but "a handful" and bore "no proportion" to the numbers of the enemy.

The slipshod method by which Congress attempted to deal with every branch of the government in the country by committees brought upon him much of the work of a secretary of war and of a chief of staff. He had to send the energetic Greene to Philadelphia to stimulate the production of artillery, ammunition, wagons, and entrenching tools. Only the timely arrival of cannon and twenty-three thousand muskets from France insured his having sufficient arms for the coming campaign. British raids on Danbury and Peekskill had destroyed invaluable tentage and other equipment that had been collected at those places.

The need of more general officers for the larger army that was expected for the coming year brought difficulties still more vexing. Congress insisted that generalships should be apportioned to each state according to the number of troops it furnished. John Adams would have had the generals elected annually after the manner of ancient Greece and Rome! When Washington asked for three lieutenant generals, nine major generals, and twenty-seven brigadiers, Congress appointed no lieutenant generals at all, five major generals, and only ten brigadiers.

John Stark, deeply hurt by being passed over, was not the only distinguished veteran to resign in protest against such treatment. Washington had to dissuade Benedict Arnold from doing so. But the list was well chosen, so far as it went. The new major generals were Thomas Mifflin, Arthur St. Clair, Adam Stephen, Lord Stirling, and Benjamin Lincoln. Notable among the new brigadiers were John Glover, Anthony Wayne, and the Reverend John Peter Muhlenberg, who arrived at Morristown that spring at the head of a battalion he had recruited largely from among his congregation in Virginia.

The whole business of promotions, moreover, was soon complicated by the arrival at Morristown of a number of French, German, and Polish officers whom Silas Deane, one of the American commissioners at Paris, had accepted for service and whom Congress had accepted at face value. One such had already made a lamentable showing in the delaying action before the second battle at Trenton. In February, Washington described himself as "laid under" and, in May, as "haunted and teased to death" by "hungry adventurers, knowing not a word of English," who had conveniently lost their papers but, nevertheless, expected commissions as field officers.

Congress, impressed by the prestige of foreign military training, had made generals of four officers of the French army, and to one of these Deane had promised the post of chief of both the American artillery and engineers, with a rank superior to that of even such veteran major generals as Sullivan and Greene. Washington protested. Greene, Sullivan, and Knox, the creator of the American corps of artillery, threatened to resign. Congress rebuked all three but decided that Deane had exceeded his powers and placated the Frenchman with high rank as Inspector General of Ordinance and Military Manufactory.

A British raid on Bound Brook early in April must have been almost a welcome distraction from these nagging troubles. On Sunday, April 14, Cornwallis at the head of four thousand men who had marched through the night from New Brunswick surprised Lincoln's command at their breakfast and drove them from their blockhouse and trenches in disorder, with a loss of two guns and 60 men killed, wounded, and taken prisoner. Greene's division marched as promptly as possible the twelve miles from Basking Ridge to support them. But by the time it arrived the British had destroyed considerable supplies and they retired with about a hundred captured sheep and cattle and other booty.

Washington was still writing that, unless the new organizations came in faster than he saw reason to expect, the campaign would open without men on the American side; that no troops had joined him from New England, few from the south; and that "langor and supineness" prevailed everywhere. Congress had a way of disposing of troops without consulting their Commander in Chief or even letting him know what had been done with them. Some of the orders of the state governors he called "ridiculous and inconsistent."

It was the twentieth of May before Knox could write to his wife: "Our forces come in pretty fast and are disciplining for war . . . well supplied with arms and ammunition of all kinds." But while the table of organization provided for 42 regiments, grouped in five divisions of two brigades each, the officers and men present for duty at Morristown numbered only 8378, and among these there were counted some short-term militiamen.

With the coming of spring, Washington's secret service had informed him that more troops from Newport had arrived at Perth Amboy. The troops there and at New Brunswick had been moved from their crowded quarters and placed under canvas along with those Hessians who, for want of shelter on shore, had been existing miserably aboard the transports that had brought them from Newport in February. Early in May the sick and wounded, the camp women, and other non-combatants had been evacuated.

At New York the construction of flatboats suitable for landing operations and the presence of 70 transports, several of them with horse stalls lined with sheepskins, seemed to indicate that the enemy's next move would be an amphibious one. On the other hand, the arrival from England of a pontoon train, which might have enabled Howe to capture Philadelphia if he had had it with him on the Delaware the past December, indicated a fresh advance by land against the rebel capital. In confirmation of this a reconnaissance in force under Sir James Grant reached Bound Brook on May 26 but got no farther. In the ensuing skirmish a cannon ball decapitated Grant's horse, and—as Wayne noted with satisfaction—the General was plastered with mud and badly bruised by the animal's fall.

Two days later Washington, who had been keeping his troops busy at drill and target-practice, broke up the camp at Morristown and led his army southward to the Middlebrook Valley, where he placed it in a strong position a little to the north of Bound Brook. Thence he could more quickly threaten the flank of any British advance on Philadelphia or easily march back through Morristown to Peekskill if Howe should move up the Hudson. And there, moreover, he could well afford to await the enemy's next move, for now his forces grew stronger every day. The New Jersey militia joined him in large numbers. The Rhode Island regiments were hastening from Peekskill to join him, and down on the Delaware the Pennsylvania militia were gathering enthusiastically, under the command of Arnold, for the defense of the river crossings, if that should become necessary.

Not until June 11 did Howe advance. And then he moved, not by the direct route to Philadelphia through Princeton and Trenton, but toward Bound Brook, as if intending to cross the Delaware at Coryell's Ferry. At the head of an army of eleven thousand troops, who were now in excellent condition, but with a baggage train of a thousand vehicles, he was continually assailed by parties of armed farmers on horseback. It took him two days to reach a point three miles beyond Somerset Court House and only 13 miles from New Brunswick, and there he remained for nearly a week, evidently in the hope that Washington would attack him. But Washington refused to be lured from his entrenchments; his position was too strong to be taken without crippling losses; and Howe dared not march on to the Delaware leaving the unbeaten American army in his rear. Meanwhile Morgan's riflemen and the neighboring farmers assailed his convoys, cut up his patrols, and nightly harassed his outposts.

Finally, on June 19 Howe pocketed his pride and retired, not only to New Brunswick but to Perth Amboy, where he began ferrying his troops to Staten Island. Greene, following swiftly, drove the Hessians out of the redoubts at New Brunswick with his division, and Stirling's had all but reached Staten Island Sound when Howe turned upon it, routed it, and pushed as far as Westfield, as if he intended to seize the mountain passes on the American line of communications to Peekskill. But Washington, confident that Howe would not involve his troops in that difficult country where the Americans would be able to do the kind of fighting they liked best, recalled his army to its Middlebrook position and there on July 4 celebrated the first birthday of the American nation by hoisting Betsy Ross' new flag over the camp.

There remained for Howe nothing but to make another inglorious retirement, his frustrated and angry men plundering and burning the houses of Tories and rebels alike as they went. This time he moved his entire force to Staten Island, evacuating all New Jersey except the post at Paulus Hook, and began embarking his troops on the transports that had been prepared for them. On July 23, escorted by Admiral Lord Howe's warships, they put to sea. A magnificent armada of 211 sail, as Washington's secret agents counted them, they bore a splendid army perfectly equipped and supplied. There were eight camp women to every hundred men, a horse for each field and staff officer and each captain, and—it was gossiped—"ammunition wives" for some of the officers.

Even Washington's secret service had failed to discover the expedition's objective. Philadelphia had seemed the most probable. But now Peekskill appeared not unlikely. For in the past few weeks General John Burgoyne, at the head of a strong force of British and Hessian regiments had been advancing up Lake Champlain with Albany, evidently, their objective, and had lately captured the American fortress at Ticonderoga. By the principles of sound strategy Howe ought to advance up the Hudson and take the forces opposing Burgoyne in the rear.

For the next four weeks Washington continued to find Howe's movements "puzzling and embarrassing beyond measure." He sent all the troops he could spare to Schuyler's command at Albany and only at the last moment decided against leading his whole force to Peekskill, when a letter from Howe to Burgoyne, promising to attack Boston, was found on a captured messenger in circumstances that made it clear that it was intended to be captured. Five days later four of Washington's five divisions were crossing into Pennsylvania by the Trenton ferry and Howell's ferry and Coryell's.

The British fleet was sighted off the Delaware Capes, but only to disappear to the eastward. Washington established his headquarters at Germantown, for the five days of hard marching in the August heat had exhausted his men. A week later the enemy fleet was reported to have been sighted 16 leagues to the south of the Delaware Capes. Was Howe aiming at Charleston in South Carolina? If so, Washington could do nothing to stop him and, still anxious for Peekskill, the keystone of the defense of the entire country, he was about to march for the Hudson when Howe's ships were reported from far up Chesapeake Bay. They would only have to sail up to the head of the bay to land their troops within a few easy marches of Philadelphia. On Sunday, August 24, Washington paraded his army through Philadelphia, and next day they were marching down the Delaware to Wilmington.

The next four weeks saw Washington outflanked and defeated at Chadds Ford on the Brandywine, his ammunition ruined by torrential rain when he was about to give battle at Warren Tavern, and Wayne's command nearly destroyed at Paoli. On September 25 Howe's army marched as deliverers into Philadelphia, from which Congress and most of the Patriot citizens had departed in good time. But although at long last Howe was in possession of the rebel capital, he found himself close to being blockaded there, his army and the civil population uncomfortably short of food.

He barely avoided being disastrously defeated by a sudden onslaught from Washington's army through the morning fog at Germantown on October 4. From a strong position a night's march to the east on Skippack Creek Washington dominated the country on the British front. Guerrillas on the Jersey shore and down the river on the Pennsylvania side made foraging difficult and dangerous. Admiral Howe's fleet and the supply ships had come around from the Chesapeake to the Delaware, but those forts that had barred the river to the British advance in August still closed it above Chester.

It took three thousand men to guard each of the wagon trains that brought supplies through the 15 miles of enemy-infested territory that lay between Philadelphia and the supply ships at Chester, and only under cover of darkness could convoys of small boats be brought up through the narrow Tinicum Channel next to the Pennsylvania shore to the mouth of the Schuylkill River without drawing the fire of the nearest fort. Before the end of October the troops at Philadelphia had to be put on half-rations. Their outposts had to be fortified with redoubts, so heavily and continually were they attacked. It became obvious that, if Howe and his army were to winter in Philadelphia, as he intended, the river must be opened to his ships.

The operation was a formidable one. A fort at Billingsport, on the Jersey shore about six miles up the river from Chester, guarded a submerged *chevaux-de-frise* of iron-pointed timbers that blocked the channel to ships of any considerable size; and when Washington had this fort abandoned and Admiral Howe's sailors had cleared the channel at that point, there remained a still stronger similar barrier a couple of miles farther on, which was dominated by the guns of Fort Mifflin on Great Mud Island. A little beyond that, Fort Mercer on the heights at Red Bank on the Jersey shore was so placed as to cover with its fire the rear of Fort Mifflin.

Neither fort had been completed, but Mifflin's lofty stone redoubt withstood a whole day's bombardment by the British warships, and British headquarters at Philadelphia decided that the quickest way to capture it was to take Mercer and turn its guns on Mifflin's rear. Von Donop, who had lately arrived from New York at the head of four thousand Hessians and was anxious to clear their record of the stain that their comrades had placed upon it at Trenton, begged for the privilege of making the attack.

Marching by way of Haddonfield, he led two thousand of them against the fort on the morning of October 21. There were only four hundred Rhode Island troops to defend it, a number totally inadequate to man its extensive ramparts. But Colonel Christopher Greene, their commander, hoisted his flag on a tall hickory tree, concentrated his force in a small pentagonal redoubt in the center of the works; and from its parapet his men poured so deadly a short-range musketry fire upon the charging enemy that after 40 minutes four hundred of the Hessians lay dead or wounded, including three of their colonels and a score of other officers. Von Donop, mortally wounded and made prisoner, grimly reminded his captors that he had promised them "no quarter," when Colonel Greene refused to surrender before the attack.

While the attack was in progress the British warships seized the opportunity to assail Fort Mifflin with their heavy guns. But they were beaten off with heavy loss.

H.M.S. *Augusta,* a 64-gun ship-of-the-line, ran aground, took fire, and blew up. The 18-gun cruiser *Merlin* also grounded and under a hail of American shot and shell had to be set on fire and abandoned.

To add to the depression caused by these reverses a rumor filtered through from Washington's army that they were celebrating the news that up at Saratoga Burgoyne's army had been forced to surrender. The British refused to believe it at first. But true or false, the forts on the Delaware had to be taken or Howe would have to make still another discreditable retirement. By early November the troops in Philadelphia were running short of rum, clothes, and even of ammunition; there was neither meat nor fowl to be seen in the markets, and very few vegetables. It was now evident, moreover, that only by the slow and laborious process of a regular siege could Fort Mifflin be taken.

The guns of the fort prevented any work on the English siege batteries except at night. The weather turned foul, and a howling northwest wind brought ice a half-inch thick. But batteries were built on the adjacent islands and armed with 32-pounders from the warships, and on November 10 the bombardment began. Five land batteries of heavy howitzers added their fire to that of the naval guns and a 13-inch mortar from the fleet at a range of only 600 yards. Six ships-of-the-line cannonaded the fort at 900 yards. It sounded like a continual thunderstorm day and night to one Hessian officer.

In the fort three hundred Maryland troops and half as many Pennsylvanians from Washington's army replied with equal fury and repaired at night, so far as possible, the damage done by the enemy's bombardment during the day. Their fire swept the crew from a great floating battery and sent 34 cannon balls through H.M.S. *Isis* from side to side. Their total casualties amounted to two hundred and fifty—four hundred according to the

British—and reinforcements and labor gangs of militia had to be sent in every night. But on the sixth day of the bombardment their last cannon was dismounted, and one of the most brilliant, and little known, episodes in American military history came to an end. That night what was left of the garrison, leaving their flag flying, slipped away across the river and joined Colonel Greene's command at Fort Mercer.

Washington, obliged to maintain a position between Howe's army and the American supply depots at Easton, Bethlehem, and Allentown, had been unable to move to the relief of Fort Mifflin. He had, however, advanced to Whitemarsh, whence he could see the smoke of the British outposts at Germantown. When he heard that upon the evacuation of Fort Mifflin Cornwallis was advancing with 5500 men upriver against Fort Mercer, he sent General Nathanael Greene, with one-third of the troops at Whitemarsh, to aid in its defense. But down at Mercer, Colonel Christopher Greene, ignorant of the approach of this assistance, evacuated the fort on the very day on which the General and his troops left Whitemarsh. Cornwallis' troops turned to foraging, and the General could do no more than press them closely as they retired to the ships that had been sent to take them back to Philadelphia.

On December 4 Howe marched out against Washington's position at Whitemarsh. But three days of probing the line of entrenchments that crowned heights bristling with abatis convinced him that an assault, even if it were successful, would be too costly—he had never forgotten the lesson taught by Bunker Hill—and he marched back to Philadelphia on the seventh, so closely followed by Washington's light troops that every hilltop became the scene of a rear-guard action.

Four days later Washington began the series of marches that brought his army on December 18 to Valley Forge, to the end of one of the most arduous campaigns in the history of their country, and to the beginning of an ordeal of hunger, cold, and misery that was to become proverbial.

IV

THE MAKING OF AN ARMY

ALTHOUGH HOWE'S SEABORNE EXPEDITION against Philadelphia had shifted the war's principal theater of operations to Pennsylvania, it was far from leaving peace in New Jersey. In late August Sullivan, whose division Washington had left behind him, led it in a bungled raid on the British posts on Staten Island. Sir Henry Clinton, to whom Howe had committed the command of what Sir Henry called a "damned starved defensive" at New York, had relieved his frustration in mid-September by raids into Bergen and Essex counties which kept a considerable number of the New Jersey militia from marching to reinforce Washington's army. In October Washington had sent home some nine hundred of them as having done their full duty. But Governor Livingston had sent a thousand of them to support Putnam in the Highlands that month, when Clinton raided up the Hudson and burned the town of Kingston, New York.

In West Jersey, where the Tories were numerous and active, the Patriot militia turned out reluctantly to assist in the defense of the forts on the Delaware, although Washington had begged Governor Livingston for all the help that New Jersey could give. Those who answered the call were entirely unsuited to the desperate character of the fighting in Fort Mifflin, but they rendered invaluable service in labor gangs that were ferried over to the fort each night to repair the damage done by each day's bombardment. A Continental detachment under Brigadier General James Mitchell Varnum supplied shoes and clothing to the Continental troops by collecting them from the Tory Quakers in Salem: their orders were to act "with Humanity and Tenderness; But at all Events, to procure the Articles necessary for the Garrisons."

Upon the loss of the forts Washington had ordered the destruction of Commodore Hazelwood's squadron of the Pennsylvania Navy that had contributed so greatly, though inconspicuously, to the security of the troops opposite Trenton in the dark weeks of the previous December. Discouraged by the loss of Philadelphia, a good many of the men had deserted; many of the rest were not to be relied upon; and there was a severe shortage of ammunition. But with the five galleys and five small boats he could man, Hazelwood had done what was possible until the destruction of Fort Mercer rendered his vessels useless. On the night of November 21 some of them managed to slip past the batteries at Philadelphia and reach their base at Bordentown. Others were set on fire at Gloucester and burned until the explosion of their magazines blew them to pieces. To Hazelwood, to Colonel Samuel Smith, and to Colonel Christopher Greene, the commanders of the two forts, Congress voted "elegant presentation swords" in recognition of their services.

The crews of the destroyed and dismantled vessels could only with difficulty find quarters in Trenton, where the damage done in last winter's battle had not yet been completely repaired. The town was soon still further overcrowded by the arrival of the light cavalry that, owing to the dearth of forage nearer at hand, Washington had sent over from Valley Forge. Under the command of the celebrated Polish exile Count Casimir Pulaski their scouting had been invaluable in the marches that followed the battle at Chadds Ford, and they were now useful in keeping the country around Trenton clear of the gangs of Tories and outlaws that infested the Jersey side of the Delaware to the southward.

Washington had forbidden the sale of supplies and forage to the enemy, but where he had no power to enforce his order the inhabitants ignored it. The West Jersey people near Philadelphia traded openly with the British in the city. Down at Haddonfield Captain Henry Lee's troop of light horse gave a measure of protection to the Patriots in the neighborhood. But when they were withdrawn for more pressing duty with the main army, a Tory organization, the West Jersey Volunteers, who occupied Billingsport under the command of a former Gloucester tavern-keeper, found nothing to oppose their depredations but such small armed parties as the comparatively few Patriots in the district could rally from time to time for mutual defense.

In the February of the new year the Patriots had the sour satisfaction of seeing their Tory neighbors given a taste of their own medicine. In a foraging expedition from Valley Forge Wayne swept the district between New Salem and Mount Holly, burning the Tories' hay, since he could find no wagons with which to remove it, and driving off their cattle and horses with a thoroughness that earned him the name of Wayne the Drover. But, when he had gone, British regulars and Loyalist troops ranged the country, burning and plundering in midnight raids. As time went on, the normal way of life disappeared completely. Pastor Colin of Swedesboro wrote. "Everywhere distrust, fear, hatred, and abominable selfishness. . . . Parents and children, brothers and sisters, wife and husband, were enemies to one another."

Up in the north the British at Paulus Hook and on Staten Island dominated the southern section of Bergen County. There the occasional raiding by Patriot militia had the commendable object of breaking up trade with the enemy, but the raiders were frequently guilty of outrages like those in the Salem country. Along the coast three hundred militiamen labored in vain to suppress the shipment of supplies to the enemy at Perth Amboy and on Staten Island and the circulation of their secret agents.

Continental troops continued to garrison the fortifications at Princeton. The State legislature had again met there in the fall of 1777. When it was not in session Governor Livingston and a Committee of Safety, sitting in various parts of the State, governed as best they could, which, naturally, was not too well. They were charged with slackness in dealing with enemy spies, of mismanagement of the militia, and of stinting them of supplies. In February, 1778, in reply to Washington's urgent plea for wagons to haul provisions to his half-starved troops at Valley Forge, Livingston was moved to write: "It is impossible for this State to cure the blunders of those whose business it is to provide the army; and considering what New Jersey has suffered by the war, I am justly certain it cannot hold out another year if the rest will not furnish their proportionable share of Provisions." The State courts also drew criticism. The haste and scanty notice with which the forfeited estates of refugee Tories were sold were often such as to excite suspicion of gross irregularities.

Washington's conduct of the war drew bitter and general criticism. Patriot propaganda credited him with sixty thousand men. Why, then, had he allowed the Delaware forts to fall? Why keep his army stuck in the frozen mud and snow at Valley Forge, while its officers caroused in luxury at York? Actually, at Valley Forge that January, he was containing Howe's army of 19,530 men with a force of 11,800, on paper, of whom only 8200 were effectives; and often a third of those were sick. There were days when, if Howe had chosen to attack him, Washington's troops were too few to line even his incomplete entrenchments.

But the wonder was that there were any men at all. Baron deKalb, of the French army, whom Congress had made a major general in the past November and who had commanded a division since then, said that no European troops would have endured such hardships as theirs. In their log cabins—which were, to be sure, a great improvement over the brushwood shelters in which they had been living throughout the fall—they stuck it out, though for days at a time their only food was "fire cake and water" and the state of their clothing became so notorious that the Tory *New York Gazette and Daily Messenger* jeered that the Continental Congress could get plenty of rags for their paper money from the troops at Valley Forge. The two log-cabin hospitals were constantly overcrowded, the General Hospital at the little Moravian settlement at Bethlehem so overcrowded and filthy that Dr. Benjamin Rush, the physician general of the army's medical department, resigned in disgust. But there was only one threat of mutiny: when a couple of battalions refused to march until they were fed. Desertions were numerous, but they were mostly by men who, with their homes nearby, could see no use in staying in the camp when there was no fighting to be done, and who intended to return as soon as fighting began again.

The bitterest feature of the situation was the fact that most of this privation and destitution was unnecessary, that there was a sufficiency of almost everything available, and that only the departmental confusion caused by the ineptitude of Congress was responsible for the shortages in the camp. Reluctant as Washington was to arouse feelings against the army and the cause by making use of his dictatorial powers, a complete breakdown of the regular services of supply in February forced him to send out strong foraging expeditions—one under Wayne in the Mount Holly–Salem country, and one under Greene along the Brandywine—making payment with certificates drawn on the Commissary and Quartermaster departments as Congress had empowered him to do.

Meanwhile, wrote Surgeon Albigense Waldo, the men at Valley Forge labored through mud and cold with songs on their lips extolling War and Washington. They knew right well that Congress was to blame for their unnecessary miseries. But at York, in Congress, with often only 16 or 17 members present, and these mostly undistinguished, criticism of the Commander in Chief ran high, and it was loudly echoed at Reading by the Patriot families from Philadelphia who had taken refuge there. Forgotten was his ridding New Jersey of the British without fighting a battle. The defeat at Chadds Ford, the loss of the Delaware forts, and the inactivity of his army since then were emphasized. Ignored were the facts that the influence of Howe's army extended little beyond its outposts, that its supplies had to be brought from New York by sea, and that its supply ships, frequently the targets of Smallwood's guns at Wilmington, were often the prey of armed parties in small boats that fell upon them by night.

People who ought to have known better made slighting comparisons between Washington's record and that of General Horatio Gates, the vanquisher of Burgoyne in October, by grace of the courage and initiative of Benedict Arnold. By the end of January Washington was aware that a malignant faction had formed against him. In his own army General Thomas Conway, an Irishman from the French army, whom Congress had made a major general, and inspector general over Washington's protest, was so active in the campaign of detraction that for more than a hundred years it bore the name of the "Conway Cabal."

The disgruntled Mifflin, Colonel Aaron Burr, naturally enough, and Colonel James Wilkinson had a part in it. All fall the brew had been simmering. Patrick Henry was one of many who received anonymous letters blaming Washington for everything from the depreciation of the currency to the loss of the Delaware forts. He sent his on to Washington. John Laurens did the same with an unsigned pamphlet of similar content, called "Thoughts of a Freeman."

Upon Conway's promotion, Congress created a Board of War, with Gates at its head, Wilkinson, his confidential aide-de-camp, as its secretary, and Mifflin its most influential member. It is small wonder that in painting Washington's portrait that winter John Trumbull showed a man aged beyond his years by care and anxiety, and that Charles Willson Peale gave his eyes a shrewdly watchful if not quite cynical glance. An effort was made to win even Lafayette's support from him. It was late January before Wilkinson's tipsy babbling at Lord Stirling's dinner table about a letter in which Conway had written to Gates, "Heaven has been determined to save your country, or a weak General and bad counselors would have ruined it," gave Washington the opportunity to bring the matter into the open. The reaction was such that in the next few weeks Conway found himself snubbed by Congress, his resignation—which he had tendered as a mere gesture—accepted; and in July Cadwalader "stopped his lying mouth" in a duel, with a bullet through mouth and neck that sent him back to France.

The arrival of Mrs. Washington at Valley Forge in mid-February did much to relax the tension around headquarters, as it had done at Morristown the previous year.

The Potts house where he had been living and working, crowded in with the members of his staff, she turned into something like a home, his aides finding quarters elsewhere; and she managed the building of a cabin adjoining the house, in which the headquarters mess could dine in comfort and she could hold social gatherings such as the dinner she gave to celebrate her husband's forty-sixth birthday.

Mrs. Greene, Lady Stirling and "Lady Kitty" Alexander, Mrs. Knox, Mrs. Clement Biddle, and other officers' wives found lodgings in the neighborhood and joined her in making the evenings gay with dancing, coffee, and conversation, although they had often spent the afternoons on foot among the soldiers' cabins with baskets of comforts for those who needed them most. Hamilton's, John Laurens', and Mrs. Greene's knowledge of French helped to alleviate the homesickness of the numerous French officers with the army.

But March brought what turned out to be the best news that had come from Valley Forge thus far. It was of the arrival there of Frederick William Augustus Henry, Baron von Steuben, bearing letters from Benjamin Franklin, who described him as a former lieutenant general in the service of Frederick the Great. Actually, he had been a lieutenant quartermaster general in a class of 13 trained by the King himself. A veteran of the Seven Years' War, wounded in the battles of Prague and Kunersdorf, he wrote the splendid star of the Baden Durlach Order of Merit. He had worn a scarlet uniform turned up with blue, which he supposed to be in accordance with American army regulations, when he landed at Portsmouth, New Hampshire in December, 1777, accompanied by a staff of three and his Italian greyhound "Azor."

Since then he had evidently used his time to good advantage. He spoke English well enough to understand what was said to him and to make himself understood, and, when he paid his respects to the Congress at York, he was evidently so well aware of the discord prevailing in the American service that he politely declined an offer of quarters in Gates' house there. To Washington he wrote that he came as a volunteer indifferent to rank, and that, having served under Frederick the Great, he would serve under nobody else but Washington. Washington rode out several miles from the camp at Valley Forge to meet him. With Hamilton to help them over the language difficulty, the two men took to each other at once. Spontaneously genial and naturally kind and considerate, von Steuben quickly won the liking and confidence of officers and men.

Prussian though he was, he was shocked by the amount of work that was required of the enlisted men before their breakfast and by the superfluous numbers of them that were detailed to brigade and division headquarters and to officers as servants. His earliest service in Germany, with a *Frei Corps* of volunteers, had given him experience of such soldiers; and Washington, recognizing in him both the temperament and the professional qualifications for the task, soon had him at work on a plan for the uniform training of the army, some regiments of which had thus far been drilled by the French regulations, some by the British, and some by the Prussian.

With only two months for the task, if hostilities should recommence at the beginning of May as they must be expected to do, von Steuben wrote, in French, a drill book based on the Prussian system but confined strictly to essentials. A translation of it into military English by Laurens and Hamilton was reproduced by numerous copyists in sufficient numbers to be distributed throughout the army in weekly installments. The Commander in Chief's Guard of 60 soldiers became the nucleus for training a hundred men at a time, who then went back to aid in the training of their own units. Within a month the whole army was drilling by the new regulations, with emphasis on loading and firing, the use of the bayonet, in which American troops had always been weak, and such essential foot movements as changing from column into line, their failure in the execution of which had prevented their deployment in time to meet Howe's flanking movement at Chadds Ford.

With Washington's strong cooperation, personal cleanliness, soldierly smartness, and punctuality became von Steuben's next objectives. Non-commissioned officers were held responsible for the appearance of their men. A school for adjutants was established. But when it came to sanitation, Washington appears to have felt that tact should be used, for in mid-April in a General Order he "requested" attention to the subject "for the last time." He noted with pleasure the respect that some brigadiers had paid to similar orders in the past and wished it had been general, "but the case was otherwise." By the end of that month, however, Surgeon Waldo was writing:

> All with clothes and powdered hair
> For sport and duty do appear,
> Here squads in martial exercise,
> There whole brigades in order rise.
>
> . . . .
>
> Where all the varying glitters show
> Of guns and bayonets polished bright.
>
> . . . .
>
> One choix of Fives are earnest here,
> Another furious at cricket there.

May Day was dedicated to "mirth and jollity." Every regiment had a May Pole. Washington joined his officers in a game of cricket.

Of course, this near-miracle of transforming what was

little better than a half-starved, half-naked rabble into a smart and disciplined army in less than two months could not have been accomplished by von Steuben alone. About the time he undertook the task, Congress saw some of the errors of its ways regarding the services of supply. General Greene reluctantly accepted the position of quartermaster general and, with powers that had been denied his predecessor, reorganized the transport service and soon had the clothing and equipment that was lying dispersed in abandoned wagons all over the country brought to Valley Forge. Colonel Jeremiah Wadsworth, with authority that Joseph Trumbull had never enjoyed as Commissary General, and with transport furnished by Greene, began fairly regular delivery of adequate supplies of food.

In New Jersey the Patriots, already happy in the good news of the regeneration of the army, had further cause for rejoicing in April on the appearance of handbills offering generous peace terms that were based on certain Conciliation Bills voted by Lord North's government: clear evidence, it seemed, of the enemy's discouragement. Peace Commissioners were already on their way to Philadelphia. And the end of April brought the news that France had signed a treaty of alliance with the United States which could mean nothing less than war between France and Great Britain.

At Valley Forge the event was celebrated with a grand review, a triple salute of thirteen guns, running fires by the infantry, and huzzas for the King of France, the Friendly European Powers, and the American States. Then the officers, their ladies, and civilian guests marched, thirteen abreast, to a banquet of fifteen hundred covers, and the enlisted men enjoyed an extra noggin of rum. Two soldiers under sentence of death were pardoned, and a spy, though caught in the act, was sent back to Philadelphia with what must have been bad news for his employers.

The news that filtered through the British outpost lines was cheering also. In Paris the previous November, when a gentleman had observed that General Howe had taken Philadelphia, Benjamin Franklin had replied: "I beg your pardon, sir. Philadelphia has taken General Howe"; and time had proved him right. The winter of idleness, varied only by fatigues of shoveling snow and collecting firewood and occasional foraging expeditions, had corrupted the rank and file. The Hessians had taken to looting, and their billets only excelled the rest in a filthiness that stank to heaven in the first warm spring sunshine.

The sophisticated hospitality of the Loyalists and wealthy Quaker citizens, weekly balls at Smith's City Tavern, and the plays the officers gave at the shabby little playhouse on South Street were not enough to break the monotony of life for many of them; and their commander in chief, with his "flashing blonde" and his play for high stakes in New York the previous winter, had set them an example that had become notorious.

Living comfortably, at first in General Cadwalader's house and later in Richard Penn's, and sunk in a lethargy that disgusted the Loyalist citizens, Howe allowed the city to become the prey of corruption that extended even to the supplies of his troops and the management of their hospitals. Back in November he had asked for relief from his command and only awaited permission to go home. But when it came, in April, his troops, not forgetful that he had led them to victory in six pitched battles in the past three years and had generally been thoughtful of their comfort, gave his departure the setting of a triumph. A *meschianza* (Italian for "medley") it was called by the committee of wealthy field officers who organized and paid for it. The "rococo" medievalism of the tournament, and the fireworks and ball that followed it, drew sardonic smiles not only from Patriot Americans but from many in the British army as well. The festal night came to a close with the sound of musketry and cannon at the outposts: Colonel McLane and his picked force of Continental infantry and dragoons were setting fire to the abatis.

Sir Henry Clinton, who succeeded Howe as commander in chief, had already arrived. His orders were to evacuate Philadelphia and move the army back to New York. The new British plan was to restrict the war to the conquest of the South while New England and the Middle Colonies were merely to be harried with coastal raids. "A buccaneering war," people in England called it contemptuously. One of Howe's last operations was a raid up the Delaware to Bordentown, where his troops burned those vessels of Hazelwood's squadron that had taken refuge there, the storehouses, and the home of Joseph Borden, a leading Patriot.

Clinton's first action was a night attack on Lafayette's division, which Washington had stationed at Barren Hill, about halfway between Valley Forge and Philadelphia. But when the American force extricated itself from a position of great peril with an orderliness and skill that it owed to von Steuben's training, Clinton turned at once to the difficult task of getting his army of nineteen thousand men and not less than three thousand Loyalist refugees to New York.

The original order had been for the army to go by sea. But France was in the war now, with a powerful fleet known to be approaching the American coast; Lord Howe's squadron could not possibly defend all the transports if they should be scattered by a storm; and any delay in their passage would leave New York open to attack by Washington's army. So only the heavy guns, heavy baggage, and the refugees and their chattels, were put aboard the transports. The shipyards were burned; and on the night of June 17 the troops and the field guns were ferried across to the Jersey bank, where their baggage train awaited them. Their numbers, reduced now, by desertions and the dispatch by sea of two Anspach battalions that had become unreliable, to fifteen thousand, they rested a day at Haddonfield and then took the road for New York by way of Allentown.

The last of the British had no more than landed on the Jersey side of the river when some of Henry Lee's cavalry galloped through Philadelphia and down to the landing on the Pennsylvania bank. By nightfall Morgan's riflemen had occupied the city; next day General Benedict Arnold rolled up in a coach (because of a leg wound suffered at Saratoga) to assume command of the place; and on the twentieth Washington was riding eastward with his army to parallel by a march through the Jersey hills the British route some thirty miles to the south of them.

So the full tide of war was sweeping into New Jersey again. For the fourth time in eighteen months the British were retiring across the State. It was a bitter pill for the New Jersey Tories, coming as it did upon what they had heard of Howe's indifference to them—his refusing even to receive a deputation of 50 Tory gentlemen from Monmouth County in the past winter. The Patriots had allowed Clinton's army to reach Haddonfield unmolested, but it had no sooner resumed its march than the militia assailed its vanguard, felling trees across the narrow, sandy road, wrecking bridges, and ambushing it with such stubbornness that once, at least, the field guns had to be unlimbered to clear the way.

Although Clinton hanged two men for it, there was

plundering by both British and Hessians; houses were burned; and the farmers fled before the advancing column, taking their families and livestock with them. They took also the ropes and buckets from their wells and often left papers warning the enemy troops that they were going to be "burgoyned." On the single road available from Allentown the column, with its enormous train of vehicles—baggage and provision wagons, bakeries and blacksmith shops on wheels, pontoon train, and the numerous private carriages of refugees—sometimes stretched out for eight or ten miles.

Morgan's riflemen and General William Maxwell's brigade hung upon both flanks of the column, sniping and shooting up the bivouacs, while Cadwalader's Pennsylvanians harried the rear. For nine mornings running, the British and Hessians were under arms at three o'clock to spend long hours halted in the blazing sun or drenched by tropical downpours when the breakdown of a single vehicle brought the whole column to a halt. It was Friday, the twenty-sixth, and they were only some sixty miles from their starting point, when they plodded into the village of Monmouth Court House and were told that the next day was to be a day of rest.

For at Crosswicks Clinton had learned that Washington was over the Delaware and at Hopewell and thus nearer New Brunswick, Clinton's next objective, than Clinton was. Next day, at Allentown, Clinton had changed his route accordingly, taking the road to Monmouth Court House. Thence, by way of Middletown, he could reach Sandy Hook and send his army to New York on the transports. At Allentown also he reversed the order of his march, placing General Wilhelm von Knyphausen and the Hessians in the van, the British at the rear of the column, which now promised to be the principal point of danger. Next day, indeed, the advance troops of Washington's army were reported to be in force at Princeton and Cranbury, too close to the flank of the British route for comfort.

It was an excellent army of some eleven thousand men that Washington had been leading through the Jersey hills from Coryell's Ferry, the best disciplined, trained, armed and equipped, and fed that the United States had put into the field thus far. And if its uniform was not the regulation buff and blue, its men were adequately clothed in green or brown: many of them in the "rifle dress," with ruffles at neck and wrists, a dark round hat with a white cockade, and a cartridge box on a white belt over the left shoulder. Arms and equipment were uniform and excellent. Every infantryman—except the riflemen, whose weapons were not adapted to it—had a bayonet, a cutting sword, or a tomahawk, and two of the fine American flints that were worth a dozen of the European sort. There was a tent for every six men. Von Steuben's training showed in everything they did. They were self-confident, eager for the test of combat.

Washington had every confidence in their spirit and training, but at Hopewell he called one of the many councils of war with which he interspersed all his campaigns. Should he, by two or three days of rapid marching, he asked his generals, throw his army across Clinton's path and compel him to fight a battle, or should he merely counter Clinton's move by continuing his march to the Hudson. The latter course was obviously the safe one. On the other hand a decisive American victory just now might win the war. Greene, Wayne, and Lafayette all spoke earnestly for taking the offensive at once. Major General Charles Lee headed a vigorous opposition to it.

Since his return to the army through an exchange of prisoners in the early spring Lee had continually spoken in depreciation of Washington, as he had done in the past, and of von Steuben's transformation of the troops. Now, although few people would listen to his criticism of the general who had forced the British out of Philadelphia without fighting a battle, Lee's record on European battlefields, his quotation of the maxim of building a bridge of gold for a flying enemy, and, above all, his dwelling on the criminal folly of bringing the seasoned British veterans to bay, carried the majority of the council with him.

Washington appeared to concur in their decision. But a few hours later he had changed his mind, sent the troops under Maxwell and Morgan to participate in harassing the British column, and next day led the main body to Kingston, with an advance guard of four thousand under Lafayette at Cranbury, eight miles farther to the east, which placed him directly across Clinton's route to both New Brunswick and Amboy.

Hamilton, who had been out in front of the British column, reported to him that Clinton was now headed for Monmouth Court House; and von Steuben, who was scouting so daringly with the American light horse that both Clinton and Knyphausen identified him by his silver star of the Order of Fidelity, sent Washington a recommendation that he push forward to Hightstown immediately, thence to fall upon the British flank. But a cloudburst and a breakdown in his supply train kept Washington's forces motionless for a whole day; the British marched to Monmouth Court House unhindered and bivouacked in a position too strong to be attacked.

Next day, however, Washington pushed forward to Englishtown, with Lafayette's "flying army," as he called it, some three or four miles to the south of him, within easy striking distance of the enemy. Augmented by the troops of Maxwell, Morgan, and the others that had been hanging on the flanks of Clinton's column, Lafayette's

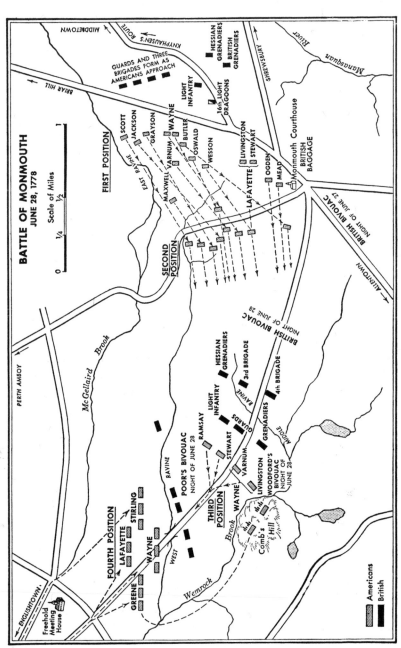

The Battle of Monmouth

From Willard M. Wallace's *Appeal to Arms*, Harper & Brothers, 1951

command now amounted to close to five thousand men, with ten guns. His orders were to attack the British troops as they followed the baggage train up the Middletown road next morning and engage them so deeply in a rear-guard action that Washington would have time to bring up his main body, defeat them, and capture the train.

General Lee, to emphasize his disapproval of the offensive movement had refused the command of the vanguard. But now, with such an important mission as this in prospect, he had the effrontery to ask for it, and to save Washington from the dilemma of snubbing either him or the senior major general of the army Lafayette relinquished it to Lee. The orders were explicit; Washington rode over that afternoon to discuss them with the general officers involved and sent them to Lee in writing that night. But when Lee's subordinates went to him for detailed instructions he gave them only surly and vague replies to their questions. Morgan, who was three miles away on the enemy's left, received no orders at all.

The result was that, although the British train began to move out behind Knyphausen's Hessians and two British brigades at four next morning, it was half-past nine when the troops under Lee's command, delayed and confused by a series of contradictory orders, deployed about a mile south of the Court House and advanced against the British rear guard, which was already in column on the road. Cornwallis, who was in command of the rear of the column, promptly deployed his troops to meet the attack. The guns on both sides went into action. The Americans were almost as numerous as the enemy before them; Wayne was not alone in thinking that he saw a good chance of victory ahead. But when Lafayette, on the American right, urged pressing their attack, Lee replied, "You do not know British soldiers. We cannot stand against them."

A few minutes later Lafayette received orders to retreat and saw with amazement that the troops on his left were falling back. To some of the brigadiers, it appeared later, Lee had said, "Take your men any place where they will be safe." Others, seeing their commands left in danger of being cut off, retired across country to the highway by which they had advanced. Lafayette's troops covered their retreat. But soon the narrow road, which led back to Englishtown, was jammed with men and guns, while the British swept forward in pursuit of them, cavalry and light artillery on the road and heavy columns of infantry on both sides of it.

"Even rout would not be too strong a word," Hamilton wrote, to describe the confusion. But there was no panic. The men were furious and sullen at "the senseless retreat," as von Steuben called it. Lee, however, refused to make a stand on the high ground between what were known as the Middle and West Ravines; and the retreat went on, with increasing disorder, until its leading elements encountered Washington, who had ridden ahead of his troops, at the bridge in the West Ravine. With a few words he stopped the flight of those within hearing and, a couple of hundred yards farther up the road, met Lee himself.

The encounter has been celebrated as the only occasion on which Washington's naturally violent temper forced him to explode in an oath. Lee, at his court martial, testified that Washington's first words to him were: "I desire to know, sir, what is the reason, whence arises this disorder and confusion." But what an enlisted man remembered was: "My God, General Lee, what are you about?" At all events, "Go to the rear, sir," Washington ordered, cutting short Lee's explanation, and himself rode forward muttering, as some believed they heard, "Damned poltroon!"

On the high ground between the two ravines Lee's

retreating troops had spread fanwise north and south of the road, with their pursuers in some places only a couple of hundred yards behind them. There Washington and his aides rallied and formed them, with their guns. It was there that twenty-two-year-old Molly Pitcher, her husband dead at her feet, dropped the bucket in which she had been carrying water to his gun, caught up his rammer and served the gun in his place.

It was an excellent position for a delaying action, and they held it, thanks to their lately acquired skill with the bayonet and Knox's finely trained artillerymen, until Washington had formed his main force of some seventy-five hundred men behind them on the farther slope of the West Ravine. Wayne's troops, with Lafayette's in support, formed the center of the new line, which was under Washington's immediate command. On his left the massed volleys of Stirling's division drove the British light infantry and the 42nd Highlanders back down the slope to the brook and struck them with the bayonet in a counter charge. On the right Greene's infantry, aided by the enfilading fire of his guns on a hill on his right flank, halted, at the marshy margin of the brook, an attack by two regiments of the line, a battalion of grenadiers, and both battalions of the Guards.

But the British held the ground where they had been stopped until the last of their eighty-cartridges-per-man had been expended. Evidently with the idea of turning a rear-guard action into a decisive battle, Clinton had sent back to Knyphausen for strong reinforcements. It was five in the afternoon when he finally ordered a withdrawal along the whole line to bivouac in a position east of the Middle Ravine.

Washington's troops moved forward across the battlefield of the early afternoon to a point where his artillery could open fire on Clinton's new position; and he was making arrangements for an attack by his whole army when darkness fell. The men of both armies were exhausted by the long hours of marching and fighting in an intense heat—the thermometer had stood at ninety-seven degrees through most of the day. Half of the British dead were reported as having died of sunstroke. The sun had struck many of the horses dead in their tracks—Washington's splendid white charger, the gift of Governor Livingston, among them.

Stretched on their cloaks on the ground, Washington and Lafayette discussed Lee's conduct until they fell asleep. Not until dawn did they or any one else in the American army learn that the British had stolen away in the midnight darkness and were too far on their road to Middletown to be overtaken before they could rejoin the rest of their army.

V

PATIENCE AND ITS REWARD

THE AMERICAN ARMY spent the next day in resting, burying the dead, and rejoicing that at long last they had defeated the British in a pitched battle. For that they had undoubtedly done. Clinton might, as he did by suppressions of fact and shifting emphasis, report it as merely a successful rear-guard action in which he had lost not a single cart. But he had called numerous troops back from Knyphausen and in the final phase of the battle committed to combat every man and gun at his disposal.

King George gave him "his highest approbation." But the Earl of Shelburne attributed what he called Clinton's "escape" to "chance and the misconduct of the enemy." Horace Walpole wrote of it, "upon the whole the Royal Army has gained an escape." It was difficult to get around the fact that victorious armies seldom steal away from the field of their victories in the middle of the night and spend the next two days in marching away from a defeated foe.

To President Laurens Washington reported: "We forced the enemy from the field and encamped on their ground," and to his brother Augustine he wrote, "from an unfortunate and bad beginning [it] turned out a glorious and happy day." Knox wrote to his wife: "Indeed upon the whole it is very splendid. The capital army of Britain defeated and obliged to retreat before the Americans."

The British losses in the battle Clinton, who shared General Howe's propensity for minimizing such figures, reported as 147 killed, 170 wounded, and 64 missing. But the American burial parties counted the corpses of 247 British enlisted men and four officers, even though the British had buried some of their dead before their departure; and including the wounded they had left behind them, they had lost a hundred men taken prisoners. The total British losses during the retreat Washington, who was never prone to exaggeration, estimated at not less than two thousand all told: more than 10 per cent of Clinton's entire strength; and three-fourths of these were Hessians who were soon back in Philadelphia, where they were cordially received. The American losses were 58 killed, 161 wounded, and 131 missing, many of whom reported later, having been overcome by the heat and lain unconscious in the thickly wooded areas of the battlefield. Seven officers were among the killed and seven more among the wounded.

The day after the battle the New Jersey militia, their time expired, marched home; Washington sent Morgan's riflemen, Maxwell's New Jersey brigade, Moylan's cavalry, and McLane's light corps to keep the retreating enemy under observation; and the following day he led the rest of his troops over the twenty miles of sandy road to New Brunswick. The intense heat disabled many of them and again killed more horses than he could spare. But Clinton would be embarking his army on the transports and might sail up the Hudson and attack the forts at Peekskill.

At New Brunswick, however, Washington gave his troops a rest of several days on the pleasant bank of the Raritan opposite the town, and they celebrated the second anniversary of their country's Independence with a salute of thirteen guns, a parade, with a sprig of green in every hat, and a *feu de joie,* which was described as "a beautiful and brilliant exhibition."

General Lee was arrested and brought to trial, as he had the insolence to request, charged with disobedience of orders, misbehavior before the enemy, and disrespect towards the Commander in Chief. The trial lasted for six weeks, the court moving with the army. Lafayette, von Steuben, and Wayne were among the 26 witnesses who testified against him; Knox headed the smaller number that appeared in his defense. He was convicted on all three counts. But the sentence was ridiculously inadequate: suspension from the service for one year; and even that was made subject to the approval of Congress, which approval Congress hesitated to give. In September Lee went to Philadelphia, evidently to exercise his personal influence on some of the members there. But in December the sentence was approved by six votes; Massachusetts and Georgia voted against it, and the votes of New Jersey, Maryland, and Virginia were divided. Retiring to his estate in western Virginia, Lee passed the most of the brief remainder of his life there in the gall of bitterness and died in a tavern in Philadelphia on October 2, 1782.

By way of Paramus (now Ridgewood) and Haverstraw the army marched slowly to King's Ferry, crossed the Hudson, and on July 24 united with Gates' command at White Plains. Thus after two years of "the strangest vicissitudes," as Washington wrote to General Nelson, the British and American armies were back at the very point from which they had set out a year before. But now it was the British who were on the defensive. The powerful French fleet of Admiral D'Estaing had anchored off Sandy Hook on July 11 and Clinton's army was busily fortifying positions on Manhattan Island, Long Island,

and Staten Island against its expected attack, for there were four thousand troops on board the French ships.

The rest of July and most of August were spent in trying to arrange a joint attack by the French and American forces, first, on New York, and, when the channel at Sandy Hook was proved to be too shallow to permit the passage of the great French men-of-war, on Newport. Sullivan was in command in that sector. He was joined by seven thousand New England militia, and Washington sent him two brigades of his Continentals with Greene and Lafayette as division commanders.

But these troops were ten days late at the rendezvous; Earl Howe's fleet appeared in the offing; and D'Estaing, fearing that he would be blockaded, re-embarked the troops he had begun to land and sailed out to meet him. Roughly handled in the ensuing battle and by a severe storm that followed it, he put into Boston for repairs and, on learning that Clinton had sent a powerful expedition against St. Lucia, sailed for the West Indies, taking the troops with him. The New England militia, disgusted by such half-hearted behavior, went home, and Sullivan and the Continentals retired to the mainland.

Washington put his troops into winter quarters that autumn in a half-circle that ran from Danbury in Connecticut through Fishkill and West Point, Ramapo and Middlebrook to Elizabeth Town. Thus he could concentrate his forces quickly whether Clinton should move up the Hudson, or against Boston, or again into New Jersey. The men were better fed, and better and more completely clad, than ever before; and although some of them were still living in tents on New Year's Day, the quarters of most of them were in huts that were soundly constructed and far more sanitary and comfortable than the hastily thrown-together cabins at Valley Forge.

Washington established his own headquarters at the Wallace house near the village of Raritan. His wife soon joined him there, and social gaieties like those at Morristown two winters before were graced by a set of new china and "six tolerably genteel but not expensive candle-sticks" that he ordered through the assistant quartermaster at Philadelphia. "Lady Kitty" Livingston and her sister, Mrs. John Jay, were frequent guests. General Greene and his wife occupied a house not far distant on the banks of the Raritan, between Bound Brook and Somerville, which she made a social center. General and Mrs. Knox had quarters near Bedminster Church. The artillery corps was stationed at Pluckemin, where a spacious room was found in which the brigade preceptor delivered a course of lectures on gunnery, tactics, and other military subjects.

The winter passed quietly. The weather was mild and fine, and the health and spirits of the men were excellent, though bad news came from the South. The British, bent on the conquest, of Georgia, had captured Savannah in December. But except for the endemic fighting along the Hackensack, there was little military movement in New Jersey or elsewhere in the North.

In October the British had raided the little ports of Chestnut Neck and Bass River, pillaging houses and burning sawmills and salt works. But along the coast as far as Cape May trade was booming. Toms River and Tuckerton Harbor, whose intricate approaches made them comparatively safe from attack, were frequently full of large ships, and enterprising businessmen hauled their cargoes by wagon to the towns inland where they sold them at enormous profit. Privateering flourished. Some thirty armed sloops out of Little Egg Harbor preyed upon the seaborn commerce in and out of New York: once they captured a transport full of Hessian soldiers; Cape May, and even New Brunswick, participated in such ventures. Shrewsbury did a lively business in supplies directly with the enemy.

As profiteering flourished, that decline of public morals that always appears in civil life in wartime became evident. In general, religion seemed to be at a low ebb. Many of the Presbyterian and Dutch churches had been destroyed, members of the former especially incurring British wrath for their conspicuous support of the revolution. But confidence in the success of the Patriot cause was now general throughout the State. At Princeton in the spring of 1778 the village had been illuminated to celebrate the news of the French Alliance. That May plans were being made for the re-opening of the College of New Jersey, Queen's College at New Brunswick, and Elizabeth Academy; and in October of the following year Princeton saw its first commencement since 1775.

The anniversary of the French Alliance was celebrated by Washington at his Headquarters with a grand ball at which he appeared in a suit of black velvet. In April, 1779, he put on a grand parade in honor of the visit of the French Ambassador, M. Gerard, who was accompanied by Señor Miralles, the Spanish agent at Philadelphia. It was June before Sir Henry Clinton moved up the Hudson and captured Stony Point and Verplanck's Landing, the terminals of King's Ferry. The Americans' new system of fortifications might well be his next objective. So Washington shifted his Headquarters to the neighborhood of Haverstraw, and finally to West Point, where, with the greater part of his forces not far off, he remained until the close of the year. He had only eight thousand of his Continentals with him now, for he had sent five thousand, under the command of Sullivan, to chastise the Indians who had perpetrated a series of massacres in the Wyoming Valley of Pennsylvania the previous summer.

In mid-July Wayne recaptured Stony Point in a brilliant night attack that yielded some six hundred prisoners and cannon appraised at one hundred fifty thousand dollars. A month later Major Henry Lee stormed the post at Paulus Hook. Governor Tryon was raiding the Connecticut shore towns from New Haven to Norwalk that summer, burning houses and shipping. An expedition of Massachusetts militia ended in disaster at Castine in Maine. Late in October a party of Queen's Rangers raided through the Raritan valley as far as Middlebrook, masquerading as Lee's Light Horse, whose uniform was similar to theirs. They burned the Dutch Reformed Church and the Somerset courthouse before New Jersey mounted militiamen nearly surrounded them and forced them to retreat. All in all, it was, as Washington said of it, "a desultory kind of a war."

Washington had spent the whole summer trying to assemble an army of twenty-five thousand men with which to cooperate with D'Estaing in an attack on New York. But the men were not forthcoming in sufficient numbers, and D'Estaing had been busy in the West Indies until October, when he had cooperated briefly with Lincoln's Continentals and militia in an attempt to recapture Savannah that cost the life of Pulaski and a total of more than eight hundred killed and wounded French and Americans.

In December Washington moved his headquarters back to Morristown and his troops to much the same positions they had held in the winter of 1777. He had only 10,400 men. The British had evacuated Newport in October, and with the arrival of reinforcements Clinton had some twenty-eight thousand under his command at New York. But although he then outnumbered Washington's army by more than two to one, he decided that the time was now ripe for completing the conquest of the South and sailed for Savannah on the day after

Christmas with a force of about eighty-five hundred British, Hessians, and Provincials.

They left a terrible winter behind them. The North River and part of New York Bay were sheeted with ice thick enough to bear the weight of artillery. The Raritan was frozen for four months. In the American army's cantonments at Morristown the snow lay two feet deep in December, and from four to six feet deep after a blizzard in January. The roads were blocked for days, and the delivery of supplies of all sorts was correspondingly confused and delayed. Clothes and shoes were again wanting. The troops went eight days without bread, vegetables, and salt. Herds of cattle got no nearer than Princeton and Newbury. Local farmers refused payment in the depreciated Continental currency. Washington's appeal to the local magistrates, however, had an excellent effect in early January: requisitions were more than filled. But it was on a hand-to-mouth basis that the army lived through the rest of the winter.

On January 14, 1780, Lord Stirling, at the head of twenty-five hundred men on sleds crossed the Kills to raid the British posts on Staten Island. They were repulsed, though not before the troops had done some pillaging. Stirling returned as much of the spoils as he could collect. But the British retaliated ten days later with a surprise attack in which they plundered shops and houses and burned the Presbyterian Church in Elizabeth Town and the academy at Newark. There was the usual interchange of raids in Essex and Bergen counties. When spring came and the troops had received no pay for five months, it became necessary to hang a few of them for desertion and a few others for robbery of civilians.

In April the new French Ambassador, the Chevalier de la Luzerne, who had succeeded Gerard, visited the army. Señor de Miralles came with him and after a brief illness died in the Ford mansion, where Washington had his headquarters. Washington made a great occasion of the funeral. A large military escort conducted the coffin to the grave in the Presbyterian burying ground; Washington, with several members of Congress, followed it; and behind him came a crowd of several thousand soldiers and civilians. Minute guns punctuated the march; a Spanish priest read a Roman Catholic burial service. Sentinels were posted at the grave, for the Spanish envoy was known to have been buried with his diamond-studded gold watch in his pocket, diamond rings on his fingers, and his coat glittering with jeweled decorations, and a nocturnal exhumation by penniless soldiers had to be guarded against.

With June came the news that Lincoln had been compelled to surrender Charleston to Clinton's army after a heroic defense. With the accompanying loss of guns, muskets, and ammunition, it was the greatest disaster ever suffered by American arms until our own times. By June 6 not a single recruit had arrived at Morristown. Washington had never before seemed so near despondency. But when Knyphausen, whom Clinton had left in command in New York, advanced on Morristown on hearing that two regiments had mutinied there, the fundamental feeling of both troops and people in New Jersey was made clearly manifest.

The farmers fired on the five thousand advancing British troops from woods and houses; the local militia turned out in force; and at the village of Springfield one of the supposedly mutinous regiments came to the support of Maxwell's brigade, which had retired thus far before Knyphausen's superior numbers. "Never did troops, either Continental or militia," Governor Livingston wrote of the action, "behave better than ours did. . . . At the middle of the night the enemy sneaked off and put their backsides to the Sound near Elizabeth Town." Their sole accomplishment had been the burning of the village of Connecticut Farms.

Returning to New York with his Charleston laurels a few days later, Clinton at once determined to wipe out the disgrace of this fiasco. With some of his troops on transports he made a feint of moving up the Hudson, while on June 23 Knyphausen again advanced on Morristown with five thousand infantry, 18 guns, and a considerable body of cavalry. Washington had started for West Point by way of Ramapo to counter Clinton's move, but Greene, whom he had left in command at Morristown, took up a strong position behind the stream at Springfield with about a thousand Continentals and a force of militia. Stubborn fighting at the two bridges over the Rahway River delayed the enemy until late in the afternoon, when Greene, his left flank threatened, retired to a strong position in front of Short Hills and there waited for the British attack. It never came. Instead of advancing, the British retired hastily in the late afternoon, leaving the village of Springfield in flames behind them. They had crossed to Staten Island by midnight, and at daylight the following day took up their bridge of boats.

Greene's losses in the action were 13 killed, 62 wounded, and 9 missing. The British losses were never accurately known but were supposed to be somewhat larger. It was the last attempt by British troops at any serious military operation in New Jersey.

But although there was no more serious fighting in the Jerseys, the next years were punctuated with events that were as trying to Patriot hearts as lost battles would have been. A new French expedition of seven ships-of-the-line and transports carrying six thousand troops under Count Rochambeau arrived at Newport in mid-July, 1780. The

British promptly blockaded them there, and Clinton would have attacked them, if Washington had not stopped him by leading his army across the Hudson at Dobbs Ferry and threatening New York by an advance toward King's Bridge. But the British fleet continued the blockade, and the French troops remained in their Newport quarters for the next eleven months.

Washington returned to his headquarters, which he had again established at West Point, and was met there by the appalling news of Major André's capture and the treason and flight of Benedict Arnold, who had been the commander of the post. There followed the harrowing business of André's trial and execution as a spy. The fortunes of the Patriot cause seemed never to have reached a lower ebb. The Continental currency had dropped in value from 40 to 1 in specie to 1000 to one and had then become worthless, and the attempt of Congress to collect supplies in kind from the states had proved in its operation, as Washington had written of it in April, "pernicious beyond description."

The army, cantoned for the approaching winter much as it had been in previous winters, from Morristown through the Highlands to Connecticut, suffered accordingly. Paid, when paid at all, in worthless paper, the men frequently went hungry; clothes again grew ragged and shoes disintegrated. Military stores, too, were in short supply. There was even a shortage of powder. At nine in the evening of New Year's Day, 1781, the six Pennsylvania regiments of Wayne's division, stationed at Morristown, mutinied. They defied with leveled bayonets the persuasions and pointed pistol of their General and, under the command of their sergeants, marched off for Philadelphia to lay their grievances before Congress.

They took with them six field guns and left behind them one of their officers dead and several wounded. But probably there was never another mutiny like theirs.

At Princeton, and again at Trenton, their discipline and individual behavior were perfect. At Princeton they turned over to Wayne, who had followed them, two emissaries whom Clinton had sent to induce them to go over to the enemy, and, after a summary court martial, assisted in hanging them as spies. At Trenton, where Washington had blocked their crossing of the Delaware with a force of one thousand men under St. Clair and where they were met by a committee of Congress and the President of Pennsylvania, they stated their grievances with forceful moderation: no pay for the past twelve months; insufficient food and clothing; and the denial of their right to honorable discharge from the service, since they had enlisted for "three years or the war" and the three years had expired. The committee promised them prompt payment of a part of what was owing them and a supply of certain specified articles; and practically all of them received their discharge. Of these, however, almost all re-enlisted within the next 20 days for the duration of the war.

In all of this Washington, naturally, had to concur. But such action could not be allowed to spread through the army. So when the three New Jersey regiments stationed at Pompton marched off for Trenton under the command of their sergeants, he had their camp at Ringwood surrounded by New England troops, who disarmed them and made them prisoners. One ringleader from each regiment was tried and convicted by summary court martial, and two of the three were hanged on the spot.

After the fall of Charleston the news that came up from the South had continued to be discouraging for the rest of the year 1780. At Camden, in South Carolina, the army of Gates, to whom Congress had given the command without consulting Washington, had been destroyed by Cornwallis on August 16, and deKalb had been mortally wounded there. The mounted Carolina frontiersmen had won a small but brilliant victory at King's Mountain in October. But at the end of the year Benedict Arnold, now a British brigadier general, had burned the town of Richmond, in Virginia.

With the beginning of the new year, however, the prospect brightened. At the Cowpens, in South Carolina, Daniel Morgan, now a brigadier general, inflicted a stunning defeat on the brilliant British cavalry leader, Sir Banastre Tarleton, on January 17. In December Washington had placed Greene in command in the South, with von Steuben second in command, and on March 15, at Guilford Court House, in North Carolina, Greene gave Cornwallis such a bloody battle that, although it was a British victory, Cornwallis' losses were such that he retired to the coast at Wilmington. Back in South Carolina again, Greene fought another losing battle, this time at Hobkirk's Hill, on April 25. But again the British losses were such that they retreated, this time to Charleston; and Greene was left free to capture or force the evacuation of the various posts by which the British had intended to secure their conquest of Georgia and South Carolina.

For, late that same month, Cornwallis led his troops into Virginia, reaching Petersburg late in May. There his junction with the British troops already in that theater of operations brought his total numbers up to 7200. Although his forces thus outnumbered those of Lafayette and Steuben, he moved so hesitantly that Wayne, who was marching from York with a force of Pennsylvania Continentals, had time to join Lafayette; and, since he had received no definite instructions from Clinton, Cornwallis retired to Yorktown, which he began to fortify as a naval station early in August.

Meanwhile, for many months, both Clinton and Washington had been sending more troops than they could well spare to the southern theater. Early that June, however, Clinton was instructing Cornwallis to return three thousand men to him. For now a new French fleet, under the command of Count de Grasse, was bound by way of the West Indies to the American coast with orders to cooperate with Rochambeau under Washington's direction. In expectation of this preponderance of French naval power for which he had been waiting for nearly a year, Rochambeau marched his troops from Newport to Providence, and thence to Dobbs Ferry, where Washington's army joined him from the Highlands on July 6.

New York was their objective. But together they numbered at most ten thousand. Clinton's forces amounted to some fourteen thousand; and his position, surrounded by its rivers and defended by strong fortifications that were supported by a large squadron of warships in the Lower Bay was too strong to be attacked until the arrival of de Grasse's fleet, which would bring with it upwards of three thousand troops and siege artillery. Then the arrival of a letter from de Grasse to Rochambeau made the prospect of a successful attack on the city even less favorable. He would sail from San Domingo for the Chesapeake on August 13, de Grasse wrote, and return on October 15, taking his troops with him.

With their time for operations around New York thus limited, Washington proposed to Rochambeau a plan, the audacity of which has seldom been equaled in military history. He and Rochambeau would march their united forces to Virginia, unite with de Grasse's forces there, and together they would capture Cornwallis' army, which Lafayette held under observation at Yorktown. The operation has been likened to Napoleon's famous march from Boulogne to Ulm in 1805, the distance, some four hundred miles, about the same.

The united forces, organized in two French and two American divisions, crossed the Hudson on August 21 and passed behind the Palisades so quietly that, covered by a vigorous feint against the British positions on Staten Island, they had reached Philadelphia, fourteen days later, before Clinton could be sure of their destination. Their march had been planned with the greatest care. Cattle were driven ahead of them, and at each halting place the troops found beef freshly slaughtered for them. Four wagons followed each regiment with its tents and baggage; two empty wagons picked up the sick and wounded of each brigade. Camp women marched on foot on penalty of losing their rations if they strayed from the column or rode in the wagons.

At long last the Jersey people could see these allies of theirs, whose idleness in the past months had diminished their own ardor for military service. They were greatly impressed by the varied and brilliant uniforms of the French soldiers and the excellence and completeness of their equipment, but still more by their perfect behavior, courtesy, and geniality. The music of their bands delighted everybody. People of substance entertained their officers hospitably where the ravages of war had left them able to do so. At Princeton Washington and Rochambeau dined at Morven with Mrs. Annis Stockton, widow of Richard Stockton, a signer of the Declaration of Independence, who had died in February.

By September 17, the allied armies, many of the troops having been brought down the Chesapeake in small vessels from de Grasse's fleet, were assembled at Williamsburg in Virginia. By October 5 Yorktown was completely invested; and, at a little past midnight on October 23, a Lieutenant Colonel Tench Tilghman, one of Washington's aides, was waking up the neighbors around High and Second Streets in Philadelphia by pounding on the door of Thomas McKean, President of the Continental Congress, with the news that Cornwallis had surrendered.

The war was over! The war was won! Or was it? In September, down at Eutaw Springs in South Carolina, Greene had, indeed, so severely crippled the British forces that they had retired to Charleston. At Yorktown the only British field army had been beaten and captured, and the fleet that should have brought it reinforcements had been so roughly handled by de Grasse that it was unable to do so until too late. The local gentlemen at Princeton gathered around a punch bowl at Beekman's Tavern to celebrate the victory. A salute of thirteen guns was fired from a fieldpiece; a public dinner was followed by thirteen toasts; and there was an illumination of the village and the College that evening. There were similar celebrations throughout the State. Washington took time out to visit his beloved Mount Vernon, where he had been able to spend but a single day since he had assumed command of the Continental army six years before. But as the months dragged by peace seemed to be still far off.

By the end of the year Washington, with the New York and New England Continentals, was back on the Hudson with headquarters at Newburgh. Wayne and the Pennsylvania Continentals had gone to reinforce Greene in the South. Rochambeau remained at Williamsburg. De Grasse had refused to join Washington in an attack on Charleston and had sailed off to the West Indies, and early in the new year came the news that Rodney's fleet had overwhelmingly defeated him in an action off Dominica. The British evacuated Charleston and Savannah, leaving New York the only important place in the United States that they still occupied. But there, under Sir Guy Carleton, who had succeeded Clinton in command, they were stronger than before.

In New Jersey Loyalist activities persisted and, stimulated by the Board of Associated Loyalists, whose president was the former governor William Franklin, increased in bitterness and cruelty. They reached a climax this spring of 1782 in the hanging of Captain Joshua Huddy, commander of a blockhouse at Toms River, in pretended retaliation for the murder of a Loyalist who had been killed after Huddy's capture. The indignation of the country boiled over; and when the British refused to deliver for execution the officer responsible for the hanging, it was decided that thirteen captured British officers should draw lots to determine which of them should pay the penalty.

The lot fell upon Captain Charles Asgill. The youngest of the group, his dismal fate aroused widespread sympathy. Sir Guy Carleton wrote to Washington, begging that the execution of the sentence might be at least delayed. While the unlucky officer lay in chains, within sight of his gallows, from May until October, the Count de Vergennes brought to bear in his favor the influence of the French court. It was pointed out that the terms of the British surrender at Yorktown expressly prohibited the treatment of captured British officers as hostages. With steadily brightening prospects of an early peace, vengeful public feeling subsided. Sir Guy Carleton broke up the Board of Loyalists. Washington wrote urgently to Congress, and on November 7 Captain Asgill was set free.

By that time political events in England had made it clear that Great Britain had no intention of going on with the war. In September there had been a brief reunion of Washington's army at Verplanck's Landing with Rochambeau's troops, who were on their way to Boston to embark for the West Indies. In the American service the prospect of discharge at the end of hostilities, accompanied, as it now was, with the fear that a Congress destitute of funds would send them home unpaid, made the soldiers increasingly restless. In October Washington sent to General Lincoln, the Secretary of War, word of this, and it was only one of his warnings to Congress of the dangers of the situation. Back in their old huts at New Windsor in December, the temper of his troops was such that he decided against leaving them for a brief holiday at Mount Vernon as he had hoped to do.

It was well that he did so. Soon after the beginning of the new year his friends became aware of the beginnings of just such another subtle anonymous attack upon his reputation as a general as had been circulated during the winter months at Valley Forge. In March he was shown copies of unsigned proposals to his officers to retire with their troops to the wilderness, leaving the Congress—and their country—at the mercy of the enemy, unless they could "obtain that redress of grievances which they seem to have solicited in vain." He promptly called together all the officers within his reach and at a meeting on March 15, which was presided over by General Gates, he proceeded, with a characteristic combination of the coldest common sense with the highest idealism, to expose the shameless duplicity of their "anonymous Addresser's" proposals. The response was a series of resolutions—passed after he had left the room—in which the assembled officers expressed their confident reliance upon the plighted faith of their country and the purity of the intentions of Congress. A week later he was writing to Lafayette: "Our present force, though small in number, is excellent in composition."

On April 6, 1783, a friendly letter from Sir Guy Carleton informed him that the preliminary articles of the treaty of peace had been signed at Paris and that King George had proclaimed a cessation of hostilities. The news was soon confirmed, and on the nineteenth, the anniversary of the battle of Lexington, Washington issued a similar proclamation. It was read at the head of every regiment, and an extra ration of rum was drunk throughout the army to "Perpetual Peace, Independence and Happiness to the United States of America."

It was November before all the troops could be discharged. But furloughs, from which it was understood that they need not return, were granted to the many privates and non-commissioned officers who asked for them. They departed in considerable discontent, for, beyond four months pay in cash, Congress could give them only promises for what was owing them. But they were well pleased by the free gift of their arms and equipment, which, at Washington's suggestion, they were allowed to take with them, and they went home peaceably.

In only one instance was the behavior of the troops sullied during these months by something of the disorder and violence that was feared. And that episode was not perpetrated by veteran Continentals who had endured the dangers and hardships of the eight years of war. At the end of June troops lately raised marched from Lancaster to Philadelphia with their sergeants in command and proceeded to attempt to enforce their demands for arrears of pay by picketing the meetings of Congress and even going so far as to lay hands upon Elias Boudinot, the President.

One consequence of their action was one of the most picturesque episodes in New Jersey history. When the Pennsylvania state government would do nothing to suppress the mutinous troops, President Boudinot transferred the meeting place of the Congress to Princeton, which thus for the next four months became the capital of the infant United States of America. A village of some seventy-five houses, it boasted several excellent inns and taverns, however, and both village and College welcomed the 22 congressmen, their families, and servants. Leading citizens crowded them into their houses; "the Library

Room" in Nassau Hall became their meeting place; students' rooms housed their committees and the War and Pay Master's Departments.

A formal visit by the French Ambassador Luzerne signalized the celebration of the Fourth of July. Washington, invited to advise Congress on the peace establishment of the army, set up his headquarters in the late Judge Berrien's spacious house at nearby Rocky Hill and on August 26, with his escort of twelve New England troopers, rode up the present-day Witherspoon Street to be cheered by the crowd and the students that packed the College yard and to be received with all due ceremony by Congress assembled in the College Prayer Hall. The reception of the Dutch ambassador at the end of October brought the episode to a brilliant conclusion. The Congressional session ended on November 1. The new Congress met on the third, and on the fourth adjourned to meet at Annapolis on the twenty-sixth; and Washington departed from Rocky Hill to make ready for the taking over of the city of New York upon its evacuation by the British, which was set for that same day.

College, village, and State viewed the departure of Congress regretfully. All three had paid dearly in advance for the distinction of having the capital of their new nation within their boundaries. Although President Witherspoon had kept Scottish prisoners of war at work for several weeks repairing the damage done by both British and American soldiers, Nassau Hall and the Presbyterian Church still bore many signs of their occupancy. In the village the blackened ruins of the Sergeant house and the east wing of "Morven" were not the only reminders of December, 1776. British armies had twice marched the length of the State and twice marched back again, leaving such ruin behind them that Sir Henry Clinton was reminded of it fourteen years later by the desolation of northern France when he rode with the Duke of Brunswick's army to the battle of Valmy.

There were wounds that went deeper and were harder to heal. A State divided against itself, many of New Jersey's counties had been continually ravaged by guerrilla warfare from the beginning of the war until the very end. New Jersey regiments were fighting each other in the Carolinas in the last of the battles in the South, as many under the British flag as under the American, according to a Loyalist historian. New Jersey, like all the states outside New England, had a large minority of Loyalists. New Jersey families were numerous among the thousands of refugees who, under the protection of Sir Guy Carleton, left the country for new homes in Nova Scotia when his army departed from New York.

Those who remained faced disfranchisement, poverty —owing to the confiscation of their property—and both social and commercial ostracism, though Governor Livingston was a leader among the many in the State who strove for tolerance and conciliation. He pardoned 17 "Tories" who had been tried and sentenced to hang for their misdeeds. It took the passage of five years and the leadership of Alexander Hamilton, Philip Schuyler, and Patrick Henry to bring about the repeal of the "Loyalist Disenfranchising Act."

BIBLIOGRAPHICAL NOTE

The reader who wishes to go further into the subject of this book, or any part of it, will find any and all of the books listed below informative and singularly interesting —beginning with the historical section of the article on New Jersey in the *Encyclopaedia Britannica,* Eleventh Edition, New York, 1911.

For life and living conditions in New Jersey shortly before and during the Revolution the following books give a comprehensive account:

The Cockpit of the Revolution, by Leonard Lundin, Princeton, 1940.

Lesser Crossroads, by Andrew D. Mellick, Jr., New Brunswick, 1948.

Historic Morristown, by Andrew Sherman, Morristown, 1905.

From Indian Trail to Iron Horse, by Wheaton J. Lane, Princeton, 1939.

The Path to Freedom, the Struggle for Self-Government in Colonial New Jersey, by Donald L. Kemmerer, Princeton, 1940.

A House Called Morven, by Alfred Hoyt Bill, Princeton, 1948.

THE MILITARY SIDE

The Revolutionary War and the Military Policy of the United States, by Francis Vinton Greene, New York, 1911.

The Secret History of the American Revolution, by Carl Van Doren, New York, 1941.

Pictorial Field Book of the Revolution, by Benson J. Lossing, New York, 1852.

The American Loyalists, Lorenzo Sabine, Boston, 1847.

English Authorship

The First American Civil War, by Henry Belcher, London, 1911.

The American Revolution, by George Otto Trevelyan, London, New York, and Bombay, 1903.

A Tory Contemporary

The History of the Origin, Progress, and Termination of the American War, by Charles Stedman, London, 1794.

The British Forces

The Command of the Howe Brothers during the American Revolution, by Troyer Steele Anderson, New York and London, 1936.

Sir Billy Howe, by Bellamy Patridge, London and New York, 1932.

American Journal, by Ambrose Serle (E. H. Tatum, ed.), San Marino, 1940.

The British Army in the American Revolution, by Edward E. Curtis, New Haven, 1926.

History of the Scots Guards, by Frederick Maurice, London, 1934.

The Hessians and Other German Auxiliaries of Great Britain in the Revolutionary War, by Edward C. Lowell, New York, 1884.

The Trenton-Princeton Campaign

Thirty Days in New Jersey, by C. C. Haven, Trenton, 1867.

The Battles of Trenton and Princeton, by William S. Stryker, Boston and New York, 1890.

"The Battle of Princeton," in *The Princeton Battle Mon-*

ument, by Thomas Jefferson Wertenbaker, Princeton, 1922.

The Campaign of Princeton, by Alfred Hoyt Bill, Princeton, 1948.

THE CAMPAIGN OF 1777, VALLEY FORGE, AND MONMOUTH

Historic Morristown, by Andrew Sherman, Morristown, 1905.

Valley Forge, the Making of an Army, by Alfred Hoyt Bill, New York, 1952.

Valley Forge, a Chronicle of American Heroism, by Frank H. Taylor, Philadelphia, 1911.

The Battle of Monmouth, by William S. Stryker (William Starr Myers, ed.), Princeton, 1927.

THE PERIOD 1779-1783

Mutiny in January, by Carl Van Doren, New York, 1943.

The Continental Congress at Princeton, by Varnum Lansing Collins, Princeton, 1908.

The following biographical works are rich in background material:

Elias Boudinot, Patriot and Statesman, 1740-1821, by George Adams Boyd, Princeton, 1952.

Benjamin Franklin, by Carl Van Doren, New York, 1938.

The Marquis de Lafayette, in the American Revolution, by Charlemagne Tower, Philadelphia, 1901.

The Life of Major General Peter Muhlenberg, by Henry A. Muhlenberg, Philadelphia, 1849.

Tom Paine, Friend of Mankind, by Hesketh Pearson, New York, 1937.

The Autobiography of Benjamin Rush, M.D., George W. Corner (ed.), Princeton, 1948.

General von Steuben, by John McAulay Palmer, New Haven, 1937.

Autobiography, Reminiscences, and Letters of John Trumbull, by John Trumbull, New York and London, 1841.

Letters of Horace Walpole, Mrs. Paget Toynbee (ed.), Oxford, 1904.

George Washington, Himself, by John C. Fitzpatrick, Indianapolis, 1933.

Writings of Washington, Worthington Chauncey Ford (ed.), New York and London, 1890.

Washington, Commander in Chief, by Thomas G. Frothingham, Boston and New York, 1930.

Washington, Savior of the States, by Rupert Hughes, New York, 1930.

Writings of Washington, Jared Sparks (ed.), Boston, 1834.

Life of Martha Washington, by Anne Hollingsworth Wharton, New York, 1897.

INDEX